GIBEON,
WHERE THE SUN
STOOD STILL

WHERE THE SUN STOOD STILL

THE DISCOVERY

OF THE BIBLICAL CITY

BY JAMES B. PRITCHARD

PRINCETON, NEW JERSEY

PRINCETON UNIVERSITY PRESS

1962

DEDICATION

TO THE MEN OF EL-JIB
WHO HAVE BORNE THE BURDEN
AND THE HEAT OF THE DAY
THROUGH FOUR SUMMERS OF DIGGING
FOR GIBEON,
WHICH LAY BENEATH THEIR FIELDS
AND ORCHARDS.

PREFACE

✸

M U C H of the history of Gibeon has been recovered through the systematic destruction of the sources themselves. When we arrived at el-Jib in 1956 to begin the first excavation of the ancient city, its remains were securely encased within sand and silt, entirely hidden and adequately protected. During four summers (1956, 1957, 1959, and 1960) we plundered layer after layer of ancient deposits for the evidence that they had preserved, we demolished walls built centuries ago in order to reach earlier buildings lying below them. Artifacts were removed from positions that they had occupied for thousands of years. Tombs were opened and depleted of their treasures, which were assigned numbers and shipped to the museums in Amman and Philadelphia for safe keeping and further study. The gaping pits from which the history of Gibeon has been dug have now mostly been filled in so that the present-day successors to the Gibeonites may continue to get their living from the soil of the ancient site.

Such depredation is the necessary price for data in archaeology. One cannot demolish a historical source—a mound of ancient ruins is as much a source for history as a rare manuscript—without assuming the obligation to replace it with a more usable record. Preliminary reports of our findings have appeared in news reports, popular magazines, and learned journals.[1] In addition to these cursory accounts two technical monographs, written primarily for archaeologists, and giving plans, drawings, photographs, and detailed descriptions, have already been published;[2] and additional

[1] See the Chronology of Preliminary Reports in the Appendix.
[2] *Hebrew Inscriptions and Stamps from Gibeon, Museum Monographs*, University of Pennsylvania, Philadelphia, 1959; *The Water*

studies, one on the tombs, and another on the winery, have been prepared for publication. These detailed reports give information which, it is hoped, will serve as a stockpile of data from which scholars in the field of the archaeology of Palestine in this and succeeding generations may draw.

This first book-length presentation of the results of our excavations at el-Jib has been written for the general reader who is concerned with the contribution that archaeology has made to the biblical history of the site. Since the book contains material not previously published, as well as the results of intensive study made since the preliminary reports were written, it is offered to the archaeologist and the biblical historian with the hope that it may be of service to them as well as to the layman.

In this presentation I have been concerned not only with the conclusions to which we have been led in the course of our excavations and studies but with the circumstances of discovery and the methods employed for extracting history from the earth. Chance, circumstances, and the human element play important roles in the fortunes of archaeology. Important discoveries have often been made because of luck in choosing the right place in which to dig. The conditions under which work is done are far from ideal. The archaeologist must make use of available labor, cope with the perils of excessive heat and disease, safeguard trees and vines as he works on land which belongs to others, and adapt primitive tools and ways to scientific procedures. In telling the story of Gibeon I have tried to show how the tale of the city unfolded week by week and year by year through excavation and study. I have sought to give in these pages a personally conducted tour, as it were, of the ruins of ancient Gibeon and what we have seen in them.

System at Gibeon, _Museum Monographs_, University of Pennsylvania, 1961.

PREFACE

The results of the excavations at el-Jib are unique in that they can be related with a high degree of certainty to specific events described in the Old Testament. For the first time in the history of scientific archaeology in the land of the Bible an actual place name of a biblical city, neatly incised on clay, has been found under circumstances which make certain the identification of the name with the ruins. This fortunate discovery of the name Gibeon at el-Jib in 1956 has made possible a new synthesis: information found in ancient sources, which have been handed down in a long religious tradition, can be linked with the archaeological data. The tangible results of the archaeologist can both measure the trustworthiness of tradition and supplement it with additional information, which for one reason or another has been rejected or neglected in the written tradition.

Chapter I contains an account of what el-Jib is like, the conditions under which we worked, and the methods that we used. Chapter II describes what is known about Gibeon from the Bible and other ancient sources and gives an account of the fortunate discovery of the link between biblical information and the remains of the ancient city at el-Jib. The most important monument discovered in the four seasons at el-Jib is the great pool. This and other features of the water system are described in Chapter III. In Chapter IV there is the account of the finding of the winery—the oldest yet known—which was capable of producing at least 25,000 gallons of wine annually. Evidence for the everyday life of the citizens of the biblical city—city walls, houses, utensils, tools, weapons, articles of personal adornment, business and commerce, cultic objects, and occupations—is presented in Chapter V. Tombs from the Bronze, Iron, and Roman Ages of occupation are described in Chapter VI. Finally, the city's history, as it can now be reconstructed on the basis of biblical and archaeological evidence, is sketched in Chapter VII.

We have learned much about ancient Gibeon from working with the men of el-Jib through four summers. For the major part of the span of fifty centuries men have lived on top of this knoblike hill rising from the broad plain. The present occupants of the hill are closely related to their predecessors by climate, water, soil, geography, and possibly by blood. Their lives have been cast in the same mold as those of the Gibeonites whom we have sought to know better. It is appropriate that this book be dedicated to the more than one hundred fifty men who have taught us much as they labored for us day after day. At a wage that is incredibly small by western standards they have worked at the task with good humor—and often with bewilderment when they saw a hole that had required weeks of their labor to dig being filled in as soon as it had been photographed and surveyed.

The first person plural pronoun appears frequently in the following pages. It is not merely an editorial "we," but a reminder that archaeological recovery is the work of a large team. In addition to the principal players—the thirty-two people who made up the scientific staff[3]—there are those who have given freely of their advice on a great variety of technical matters. Among those with whom I have discussed problems of interpretation or procedure, either in person or by letter, are the following: W. F. Albright, Maynard A. Amerine, Rudolf Anthes, Hope Athearn, Klaus Baer, Immanuel Ben Dor, Seth B. Benson, S. A. Birnbaum, Frank M. Cross, Jr., Louis deV. Day, Jr., G. L. Della Vida, R. de Vaux, David Diringer, Theodore E. Fore, Edward Gans, David Green, Jonas C. Greenfield, Alfred Kidder, II, Emil G. Kraeling, B. Francis Kukachka, Paul W. Lapp, B.

[3] See the Staff at el-Jib in the Appendix.

Mazar, George C. Miles, J. T. Milik, Sabatino Moscati, M.
Edwin O'Neill, Peter Parr, R. H. Pfeiffer, Edith Porada,
William L. Quaide, Froelich Rainey, Franz Rosenthal, Jane
W. Sammis, Brother Timothy of Mont La Salle, George
Tuma, and Wolf Wirgin. Each of these deserves our thanks
for his service. I am also indebted to R. B. Y. Scott for
suggesting that this semipopular presentation of our findings at Gibeon might appropriately be labeled by the reference to the biblical story of the sun standing still, the incident by which Gibeon is most widely identified. Harriet
Anderson, of the Princeton University Press, has contributed many helpful suggestions for improvements in the text
and for the choice of illustrations. I am grateful to her for
her assistance.

It is a happy duty to record also the help in this project
of my wife Anne, who through four summers of my absence
from home took over responsibilities which were rightfully
mine. Without her encouragement in the form of this practical assistance, it would have been impossible to write this
history of Gibeon.

Since reference is frequently made in the following pages
to the technical designations for the major archaeological
periods in the history of Palestine, we include here the approximate dates which are generally accepted for each oi
the periods:

Early Bronze	3100-2100 B.C.
Middle Bronze I	2100-1900 B.C.
Middle Bronze II	1900-1550 B.C.
Late Bronze	1550-1200 B.C.
Iron I	1200-900 B.C.
Iron II	900-550 B.C.
Persian	550-330 B.C.
Hellenistic	330-100 B.C.
Roman	100 B.C.-A.D. 300

The biblical quotations are given in the translation of the Revised Standard Version of the Bible, copyright 1946 and 1952 by the Division of Christian Education of the National Council of Churches, to whom grateful acknowledgment is made for permission to use.

The photographs are the author's with the exception of those noted below.

Only a comparatively small part of the sixteen-acre mound of ancient Gibeon has been excavated during our four seasons of work. Yet the representative areas which we have dug to bedrock have given a picture of the six cities that once stood on the natural hill. We present here what we have found and an interpretation of what these findings mean for the history of the biblical city with the hope that in time we or others who may have more developed techniques to apply to the unexcavated areas of the mound may improve upon our efforts and bring into sharper focus the history of this important city.

J.B.P.

Berkeley, California
September 8, 1961

ACKNOWLEDGMENTS FOR ILLUSTRATIONS

For permission to use the following illustrations, acknowledgment is made to:

Albert G. Flouti, for Fig. 100; A. Gaddis, for Fig. 15; L. H. Grollenberg, for Figs. 2, 3; The Metropolitan Museum of Art, for Fig. 54; The Oriental Institute of the University of Chicago, for Figs. 16, 56; A. Eric Parkinson, for Text Fig. 3; Kenneth Short, for Fig. 62.

CONTENTS

———— ❖ ————

ILLUSTRATIONS

———————— ✳ ————————

ILLUSTRATIONS

ILLUSTRATIONS

ILLUSTRATIONS

TEXT DRAWINGS

GIBEON,
WHERE THE SUN
STOOD STILL

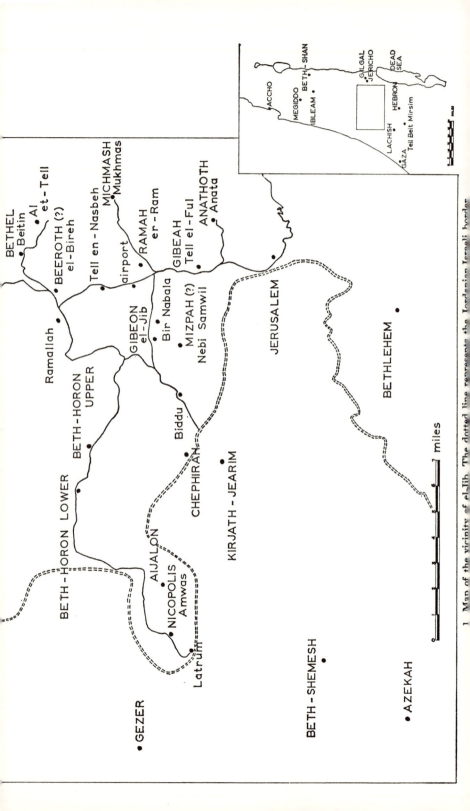

1. Map of the vicinity of el-Jib. The dotted line represents the Jordanian-Israeli border.

CHAPTER I

EL-JIB, THE SITE OF GIBEON

But none of the cities
that stood on mounds (their tell) did Israel burn. . . .
—JOSH. 11:13

T H E Arab village of el-Jib is only eight miles from the busy, cosmopolitan city of Jerusalem. Yet in the half hour that it takes to drive by car from the city to this primitive village one travels at least a thousand years backward in time. El-Jib is no suburb of Jerusalem; it is a self-contained island of the past where Arabs live today very much as they did in the Middle Ages.

The place is unmarked; one could easily pass by this modest village without being aware of its name. The only road sign reading "el-Jib" is posted two and a half miles away, where a narrow, black-top road branches off from the Jerusalem-Ramallah highway near the Jerusalem Airport. Following the direction indicated by this sign at the junction, after a ten-minute drive one comes to a rocky track on the left, over which a driver has often refused to take his taxi. This path of sharp stones winds for a quarter of a mile around the edge of the hill, past a threshing floor and two turreted guns, rusting away since the "troubles" of 1948 but still pointing menacingly toward the Israeli border only a few miles to the west, and comes to a dead end in the central square of el-Jib.

Two modest stores of one room each, a coffee house, and a mosque with a new minaret constitute the civic center of

· 3 ·

the village. The remainder of el-Jib consists of stone houses, which provide shelter for approximately one thousand Muslim Arabs and their cows, donkeys, goats, and chickens. Narrow streets, wide enough for men and loaded donkeys to pass, fan out from the village square to serve as passageways to houses and as playgrounds for children. There are no modern conveniences, such as telephones, electricity, plumbing, or sewers. A number of unused privies stand in front of houses like sentry boxes—the well-intentioned gifts of U.S. aid. Here and there one may hear the sound of a battery-operated radio blaring away at full volume.

The nearest "doctor" is a midwife in the nearby village of Bir Nabala, who not only practices her special profession but will also treat patients suffering with such ailments as a sprained leg or a boil. The village school is located a mile away from el-Jib on the main road; it is a consolidated school for four villages. Twice a day a dilapidated bus, No. 45, owned by Abed Rabbo, *mukhtar* of el-Jib, passes along the main road taking passengers to and from Jerusalem, where anything beyond the basic necessities, such as sugar, salt, tobacco, kerosene, and a few tinned goods, must be purchased. Except for this motor transportation, the occasional radio, and the ubiquitous gasoline stove, called a "primos," life at el-Jib goes on about as it did during the Crusades.

The decision to excavate at el-Jib turned on a remark of G. Lankester Harding, who was the director of the Department of Antiquities of Jordan in 1955. I had long been interested in digging at the biblical site of Ai, a city destroyed by Joshua through a clever stratagem of ambush described in Chapter 8 of the Book of Joshua. The place had been partly excavated by the French from 1933 through 1935, but work had stopped at the untimely death of the excavator, Mme. Judith Marquet-Krause. By the spring of 1955 the French had graciously conceded their rights at the site, and Harding had indicated in a letter his willingness to issue a government license for continuing the excavation at Ai. Just before leaving the United States for Jordan, I had been assured of the support of the University Museum of the University of Pennsylvania for the Ai project.

On a hot July morning I met Lankester Harding at the Palestine Archaeological Museum in Jerusalem, eager to take up where the French had left off. I told him the news of the financial backing of the Museum.

"But why then don't you find a virgin site?" he asked.

This came like a bombshell into the scheme of which I had long dreamed. Yet it did not take long to sense the advantages of this proposal. A new site would be far more exciting than one that had been partly worked.

"What about Gibeon?" I asked.

"Let's see where it is supposed to be," Harding replied.

We went into the Scrollery of the Museum, where tables and drawers were overflowing with scraps of Dead Sea scrolls, and brushed aside some bits of this precious material to get at a map of the area to the north of Jerusalem. We traced the road to el-Jib, which had long been proposed as a probable site of the biblical Gibeon. That same afternoon I hired a car, and with Monseigneur Patrick W. Skehan, director of the American School of Oriental Research in Jerusalem, I visited el-Jib for the first time.

Two promising clues were immediately apparent. One was a possible remnant of the biblical name Gibeon in the present-day name of the village, el-Jib. The other clue was a mass of broken pottery from jars of a type commonly used in the seventh century B.C. scattered on the surface among well-cultivated tomato plants and grape vines. Fortunately the modern successors to the ancient seventh-century inhabitants had moved their homes in more recent times from the area of archaeological interest and settled on the northern end of the saddle-like hill. The ancient city was unencumbered with buildings and thus readily accessible.

Little did I realize when I left el-Jib after the first visit on July 1, 1955, with pockets full of potsherds from the Iron Age, that we should soon have the luck of finding the name Gibeon in that very hill over which I had walked, that the village would become a kind of second home for four summers, and that the curious assortment of boys and men who collected around us with such obvious perplexity would eventually become some of our best workmen and staunch friends in the years ahead.

El-Jib is a pleasant place in which to work. Situated as it is 2,500 feet above sea level—about the elevation of Jerusalem—it catches the prevailing breeze from the Mediterranean, twenty-seven miles to the west, and enjoys a moderate climate even in the summer. Its latitude is roughly the same as that of El Paso, Texas. The average temperature in August is 75 degrees, the average for the same month in Philadelphia and in Washington, D.C. But unlike the eastern seaboard of the United States, el-Jib has very cool nights. Although the daytime temperature for August is 85 degrees, the average goes down to 64 degrees at night.

In the summer of 1957, when we drove out to the village from Jerusalem each morning at 5:00 A.M. to supervise the first shift of workmen in clearing the great pool, there was a familiar sight of men rising from beneath heavy quilts laid out on their threshing floors where they had spent the night beside their grain. By noon these same men were often wet with sweat as they carried baskets of debris from the pool in which we worked that season.

The average rainfall of 24 inches a year is slightly more than the normal rainfall in San Francisco; rains come from late October through the middle of May and one can be certain of five months of drought in the summer. Some pitifully small efforts are made by the farmers of el-Jib to impound the winter's rain but most of this valuable water is lost as it runs off quickly in the limestone gulches or wadies.

Sometimes there is fog in the early mornings of August —occasionally we have had to use headlights to pierce the fog which settles in the valleys along the road between Jerusalem and el-Jib—but this is quickly burned away by the morning sun. The early morning dew is an aid in the growing of such vegetables as cabbage, tomatoes, onions, squash, and cucumbers during the rainless summers.

The prevailing breeze from the Mediterranean has served as a natural air-conditioning system for our work tents, pitched on the west side or the top of the hill. The breeze is important for the economy of the village in that it is utilized in the process of threshing grain, as it probably has been for the five thousand years that men have lived on the top of the hill. Large open areas of bare rock at the northwest of the village serve as threshing floors. After the harvested grain has been spread upon the rock and trampled and pounded by oxen, cows, donkeys, or by any other animal that has hoofs, and sometimes further crushed by an iron sledge, the grain and the straw are thrown into the air with a fork. The breeze carries off the lighter material and deposits it neatly a few feet away, while the grain falls in a golden cascade beneath the winnowing fork. Farmers sleep on the threshing floor to guard their grain during the night just as Ruth and Boaz did in biblical times.

Water is scarce and its supply is carefully safeguarded, especially during the summer drought. The main spring of the village, the *ein el-beled*, which lies to the southeast of the modern settlement, has a guard day and night. The wife of our chief pottery-washer, Ibrahim, is paid by the village to ration the water from the spring; each family of the village is allowed the same amount. In the early hours of the morning one can see a steady line of women carrying water to their homes either in a large pottery jar or in a five-gallon oil tin skilfully balanced upon the head. Seven smaller springs flow from the base of the natural hill on which the ancient town stood, but these have but a niggardly flow. So narrow is the margin between supply and demand that we have been forced every year to transport by donkey from a well several miles distant from the village all the water that our laborers have used for drinking and that we have needed for washing pottery.

We have always dug at el-Jib within the months of June, July, and August, the hottest part of the Palestinian year. This seemingly odd schedule for work has been determined by factors that combine to outweigh the disadvantage of the summer heat.

First, it is possible to assemble during the summer months a staff of academic people—professors and graduate students—who are able and willing to work without salary during their vacation. About three-fourths of the thirty-two people who have worked as staff members at el-Jib over the four seasons have, during the academic term, either taught the languages, history, or literature of ancient Palestine, or have been students of one of these disciplines. In exchange for some firsthand experience in field archaeology in the area of their interest they have given their services without pay, except for board and room, and transportation for those who have had previous field experience.

A second reason for working in the summer is the availability of labor. When the grain harvest is over early in June, the village farmer has little to do. Not only are the men eager to work, but schoolboys, who are frequently more useful than men, are available during the summer holiday. Actually during the summer months we have been uncomfortable only on a few days when the westerly breeze failed, and we have been entirely free from the inconvenience of stopping work because of rain.

Success in archaeology depends largely on good planning, luck, and a staff which can cope effectively with good fortune when it appears. Since luck is, as Arabs say, "from Allah," one can only hope for it. A staff, however, must be picked with care.

The core of any staff consists of the supervisors, people who can act as foremen over from ten to twenty workmen and at the same time recognize and record what the workmen turn up. Generally a supervisor is responsible for a plot which measures 5 meters (about 16 feet) square. His crew generally consists of one skilled pickman, three men with hoes, nine basket boys, and one highly trained man who works only with trowel, hand pick, or brush (Fig. 12). These men must be organized to work as a team. The supervisor must deal with the personal problems of his laborers, such as laziness, illness, cut hands and feet, fights, and other emergencies which arise more frequently than one might imagine; he must see to it that a supply of drinking water is always available for the men; and he must give his instructions to the men in Arabic. This disciplinary part of the supervisor's job is not unlike that of a junior high school teacher.

In addition to this obvious responsibility the supervisor must see to it that every piece of pottery and other small finds are collected in a basket which is accurately labeled with the date, plot number, depth, and notations of floor levels or other fixed points. He must make a diagram in his notebook, where all observations are recorded, of every wall or heap of stones found. A good supervisor must know what to look for and recognize significant evidence when it appears. He must be neither a timid digger nor a rash one who removes carelessly evidence that can never again be salvaged. Judgment, skill, knowledge, patience, tact, firmness, and an understanding of human nature—these are some of the essentials.

Among the veterans who have helped with supervision are Fred V. Winnett and Diana Kirkbride, each of whom has directed his own excavation; William L. Reed, H. Neil Richardson, Arnulf Kuschke, John L. McKenzie, Linda A. Witherill, Robert H. Smith, Hasan Mamluk, and Mohammed Hasan, who can count up an impressive number of excavations on which they have worked. Our surveyor, Subhi Muhtadi, has been at el-Jib for the four seasons; Asia G. Halaby has worked on every expedition except the first; and Gustav Materna has been draftsman for the last two seasons. In addition to this experienced help we have had the service of many others who have been quick to learn archaeological methods.[1]

Recording is the most time-consuming chore of archaeology, and perhaps the most important task. The bulk of evidence from el-Jib has been pottery; most of it has come in small pieces of handles, rims, bases, and the nondescript fragments from the bodies of vessels (Fig. 11). Every scrap of pottery is saved, washed, dried, and sorted. Two men sit all day at tubs washing sherds which have been brought from the plots in carefully labeled baskets (Fig. 10). After the washed sherds have been laid out on straw mats and allowed to dry they are examined by the field cataloguer and the director, who make notes of general observations and select certain crucial and representative pieces to be catalogued. Each piece saved for the catalogue is rewashed, sometimes in a bath of dilute acid to remove limestone incrustation, and then inscribed with a serial number in India ink. The sherd is drawn to scale by a draftsman, photographed, and described as to color, hardness,

[1] A complete listing of these appears in the Appendix.

shape, etc. by the cataloguer. The description is entered on a card, of which there are two duplicates, and photographs of both the object itself and the drawing of it are attached (Fig. 4). One copy of this file of objects is given to the Department of Antiquities; the other two copies are used in the writing of the final report of the results of the excavation. From the card file one can see at a glance what a bit of evidence is, where it came from, when it was found, and whose notebook records the plan and the description of the find. Essentially the same procedure is followed in recording the other small finds, such as metal objects, bone, stone, jewelry, coins, glass, and other relics of ancient culture.

A considerable variety of specialized skills is called for in scientific excavation. The roles of the photographer, the draftsman, and the cataloguer are obvious. The work of the surveyor is important from the very beginning, since it is he who must plan the attack upon the ancient city.

Our surveyor, Subhi Muhtadi, who once served as city planner for the rapidly growing city of Jericho, first laid out the lines to which we were later to relate every discovery. Reference points were marked by means of iron rods set in cement at several high positions on the mound. Muhtadi then made a contour map of the entire hill and overlaid it with grid lines which divided the site into areas that measure 100 meters square (Text Fig. 2). By reference to the fixed points these areas of the map can be staked out on the ground from year to year. Each of these thirty-six areas were given an Arabic "area number," which can be written on every object from that area. The area was then subdivided into 400 plots that are 5 meters square and each of these plots was given a number (north-south) and a letter (east-west). Whenever an area is to be excavated, the surveyor drives wooden stakes, which are painted with the proper grid designations, into the ground at the corner

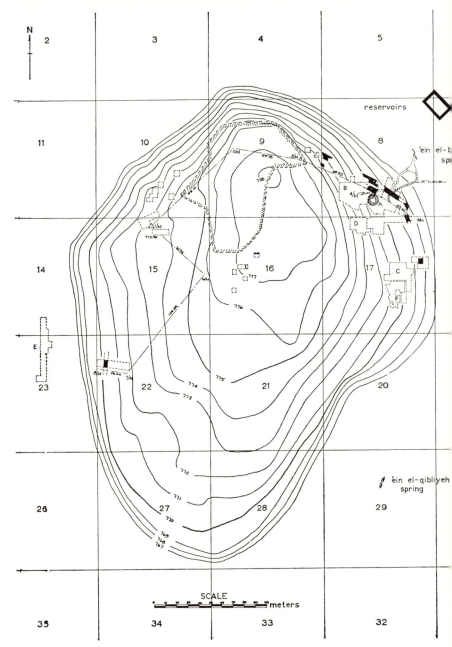

N

2   3   4   5

reservoirs

11   10   9   8   'ein el-b
                              sp

B

14   15   16   17

E

23   22   21   20

'ein el-qibliyeh
spring

26   27   28   29

SCALE
meters

35   34   33   32

2. Contour map of the hill at el-Jib, overlaid with grid of 100-meter squares.
Dotted lines indicate the excavated areas.

of each 5-meter plot. It is the grid on the master plan of the site which serves to tie together the plans of discoveries made from season to season.

As a plot is excavated the surveyor makes a plan of each wall or rock cutting as it is unearthed. This record of the surveyor is supplemented by progress photographs that are taken at frequent intervals during excavation and by final photographs taken when the area is completely cleared of debris. The record of every 5-meter plot consists of the sketches and notes of the supervisor in his field notebook, the plans of the surveyor, and the photographic record of the various stages of the excavation (Fig. 13). From this record one should be able—if he had the patience—to put everything back into the plot just as he had found it.

Although a 5-meter plot is staked out, not all the area of the plot is actually excavated (Fig. 8). A rim of one-half meter is left untouched on each of the four sides of the square. It is as though a frame were left around the excavated picture. As the excavation proceeds the walls of dirt, or balks of unexcavated debris left between the plots, look like partitions in a large box dividing up the total contents into neat compartments. Balks serve two purposes. They make convenient runways for the basket boys who carry the dirt to the dump, and the vertical sides of the cutting provide a diagram of the floor levels and walls which have been cut through or demolished in the excavated portion of the plot (Fig. 9). Tags marked with significant information about what has been removed at various levels are attached with nails to the side of the balk. When the plot has been completely excavated, a drawing is made of the face of the balk in order to record all floor levels, lines of ash, changes in the color of the soil at various levels, and other significant details.

An overwhelming portion of the staff's time is spent in

the exacting process of recording. Except for the occasional moments of thrilling discovery, the incidents retold in popular lectures or written about in newspapers, the effort expended in excavation is as monotonous as the work of a file clerk in an office.

The University Museum of the University of Pennsylvania has been the principal sponsor of the four seasons of digging at el-Jib. Its director, Froelich Rainey, has been our main source for counsel in matters of finance and publicity. In addition to supplying almost all the money spent at el-Jib, the Museum in Philadelphia provides a permanent home in its vaults and storerooms for the excavator's share of the antiquities, and publishes both a preliminary account of each season's work and the final, scientific report in its Monograph Series.

The American School of Oriental Research in Jerusalem has been a cooperating partner. The staff has lived in the hostel of the School, a quiet place where one may have hot water for a bath on two days a week, and where there is a good archaeological library and workrooms for cleaning, repairing, cataloguing, photographing, and drawing objects. Although the accommodations are far from luxurious at the School, they are superior to those that a tent would provide at el-Jib. Only an hour a day is required for travel to and from the site. As regular as the clock, on six days of the week the northbound car has left the School at 6:30 A.M.; at the close of the work "the 3:34" has left el-Jib for Jerusalem, where members of the staff have found a welcome change of scenery in the late afternoon and evening.

In 1956 and 1957 the Church Divinity School of the Pacific, in Berkeley, California, was a joint sponsor with the Museum and secured part of the support for the first campaign. The School has generously supplied a workroom where artifacts could be prepared for publication before they were shipped to the University Museum for display and storage. The cost of the four seasons at el-Jib is difficult to estimate. In addition to about fifty thousand dollars in actual cash expended, an impressive amount of labor and services has been contributed by the men and women who have made up the scientific staff.

All archaeological work in Jordan is strictly regulated by law and supervised by the Department of Antiquities. Any ancient artifact, which is defined as anything made before A.D. 1700, in Jordanian soil is considered to be the property of the state. The Antiquity Law of 1953 specifies that "the ownership of land shall not bestow upon the owner the right to acquire the antiquities existing either on the surface or inside the land." In fact, no person, without the permission of the Minister of Education, shall "excavate, build, plant trees, quarry, burn lime or do similar work or deposit earth or refuse on or in the immediate neighborhood of a historical monument or site, or establish a cemetery on a historical site." Thus a man is prohibited from digging in his own back yard if there are antiquities in it.

Licenses are issued to persons "whose scientific competence is reasonably assured by the guarantees of learned societies or institutions." And not only must the excavator be qualified to excavate scientifically but he must publish his results within a period of two years, unless an exception has been granted because of special circumstances.

While the antiquity law of Jordan is designed primarily to safeguard the irreplaceable historical data, it is formulated so as to encourage qualified people to discover and to interpret the remains of the country's history. The holder of a license is allowed a fair share of the antiquities he finds; these objects, which are displayed eventually in the museums of other countries, are of great educational value and serve to stimulate interest in further excavation.

To comply with the provision of the law, that the Minister of Education may acquire on behalf of the government all antiquities that in his opinion are indispensable for the completeness of the Jordan Archaeological Museum in Amman, at the end of each season we have laid out on tables every object that has come from el-Jib. The "division," as the government's choice of artifacts is called, is a time of considerable anxiety. What will be taken? To see some object of beauty or of unusual historical significance tagged for the government's Museum inevitably brings a disappointment, like that which goes with losing the major game of the season. Yet in his less possessive moments the excavator knows full well that the priceless object should remain in the country of its origin.

Excavations, begun at el-Jib when G. Lankester Harding was director of the Department of Antiquities, have continued under the directorships of Said Durra and of Dr. Awni Dajani. The courtesy, helpfulness, and fairness of these men have never failed throughout the years of our work in Jordan. In addition to being able administrators Harding and Dajani are both trained archaeologists, and on their frequent visits to the site they seemed more like scientific colleagues than government officials. No happier relations could have existed between excavator and host government than those that have prevailed over the years of work at el-Jib.

A license from the government does not grant to the excavator the right to take over private property for the purpose of excavation. Land for excavation must be purchased or rented at rates agreeable to both excavator and owner. Contracts for rentals of property are usually scribbled out on a piece of paper; but even when this formality has not been observed, we have found that the word of a man is just as good as a document. Many of our agreements have been verbal and we have yet to find a man who would go back on this spoken word.

The first negotiations for land at el-Jib were the most difficult. Eight landowners reported that they had agreed on a price after several weeks of negotiations, and we met them in a government office to sign the agreement. But alas, on that very morning the Jerusalem newspaper had printed the story of the deciphering of the copper scrolls found in a cave near the Dead Sea. This text recounted how tons of ancient gold and silver lay buried in sixty caches over the Holy Land. It took considerable time to convince the landowners of the village that we had come for scientific discovery and not on a hunt for gold.

The excavator must, of course, pay compensation for the trees and crops that are destroyed. If he knew beforehand how much damage the excavation would entail and just where the walls of important structures ran under ground, agreements for rentals and damages could be signed and sealed in advance. But this is obviously impossible. Final settlements must be made when the season is over. Discussions often drag on for hours over such variable matters as the length of a vine or the height of a fig tree which has been removed weeks before. Each of six to ten landowners has his own idea about the value of his tomato plants, or vines, or fig, nut, plum, or pomegranate trees. Bargaining proceeds along the usual patterns. Voices are raised, arms waved, and a landowner leaves the room in a gesture of finality, only to return again to begin at another level of evaluation. Fortunately, in all of these exhausting sessions we have never had to resort to legal action; nor have we, as far as I know, lost a friend in many long and tedious negotiations.

There is the well-remembered case of a landowner who settled eventually for one-twentieth of the amount he had

asked originally for 365 tomato plants which he had hastily
set out in a field the night before we set up our camp for
the summer. All of this bargaining is in the good tradition
of Abraham bargaining with the Lord over the destruction
of Sodom, a case in which the patriarch was able to bring
the minimum figure down from the initial fifty to a final ten
righteous men as sufficient warrant for saving the wicked
city from destruction.

All the labor we could possibly make use of has been
readily available at el-Jib. The villagers are poor and usually
they have little opportunity for employment outside the
small chores of tending their own gardens and small farms.
Consequently there has never been a day in the four seasons
without more applicants than jobs. Rarely has there been
an absence recorded in the roll book, for when a man had
to be absent he had no difficulty in finding a brother or
cousin who would gladly answer to his name and work as
a substitute for him.

Generally we have been able to employ a force of about
a hundred workmen, who have ranged in age from ten to
eighty years. In 1956, when we began work, these boys and
men were completely unskilled in archaeological technique.
Now after four summers there is a hard core of skilled workmen at el-Jib who know what to look for and how to dig
carefully so as not to break through a floor level of an
ancient occupation or to destroy some other valuable evidence. Some have developed good eyes for sighting small
finds, such as coins and other objects. All of our workmen
have learned the value of bits of broken pottery and realize
the importance of getting these into a basket with a proper
label.

The system of paying *bakshish*, or a bonus, for every
object of special importance which a workman finds has
helped to sharpen the eyes of the men and taught them the

value of digging with care. Sometimes the reward for a single find is equal to an entire day's wage. Once when we were offering too high a rate for finding inscribed jar handles, a workman took the pains to scratch with a screwdriver what he thought to be an archaic Hebrew inscription on the smooth surface of a handle. Fortunately the forgery was easily detected, and the man was dismissed for his dishonesty. The *bakshish* for coins, for example, must be calculated carefully. If the reward is too high, coins are brought in from outside and "salted" in the excavation; but if the bonus is too low, the coins are kept by the workmen and disposed of elsewhere for more money. The *bakshish* system is a battle of wits, but on the whole I am sure that it has saved for the record many objects which otherwise would have been lost to us.

Some jobs require special aptitudes and unusual care. Pottery washers must be constantly alert not to mix sherds from different areas and levels or to lose labels. The loss of a single tag tied to a crucial basket of evidence renders the labor of digging for these sherds completely useless. The day guard at the tent is responsible for all equipment, such as picks, hoes, baskets, trowels, brushes, plumb bobs, levels, which must be dispensed to the workman and then checked in again at the close of the day. Our day guard, Shukri Abd el-Hamid, has rarely lost a piece of equipment. He has become the major domo of the staff tent, dealing out with fairness the sandwiches that are brought each day for the staff's lunch. A night guard is also required. He must be not only honest but strong and brave enough to deal effectively with the culprits in the event of an attempted robbery during the night.

El-Jib has two *mukhtars*, or mayors, bearing jointly the responsibility for law and order in the village. Abed Rabbo, the elder of the two, has aided our expedition in making arrangements with landowners and in settling disputes be-tween workmen. Jamil Ismail Jabr, the second *mukhtar*, has been for two years on the pay roll of the expedition in an advisory capacity. Faithful to the pattern of Arab hospitality he has not missed a day during two full seasons in sending both tea and coffee to the staff at noon.

In preparation for pay day, which comes regularly on Saturday, the paymaster must provide himself with bags of coins for making exact change. We have found that the best sources for quantities of coins are the cinemas of Jerusalem. At the close of the work on Saturday the men are admitted one by one to the staff tent, where they are paid and then asked to sign the pay sheet or to leave a thumb print beside the name. Not infrequently is the workman met at the tent door by the shopkeeper, the coffee house owner, the tax collector, or all three, to whom he owes a part of his week's wage.

In addition to the laborers we have recruited from el-Jib, each season we have brought five or six men from Jericho to work as trowel men. These men have had a number of years of experience in British excavations at Jericho and know better than most how to recognize a floor level when it shows up. They have been a most valuable adjunct to the working force.

Before proceeding to describe the principal results of our four seasons of work at el-Jib something must be said about the aims and motives of archaeological research. Why does one pry into the secrets of the unwritten past, looking for clues to history in the mounds of ruins and rubble?

Archaeology, like much historical research, is concerned with the discovery of evidence for people in some respects very much like us. Although potsherds, walls, strata, and the other relics that the archaeologist finds are all inanimate things, it does not require much imagination to see that some real and living people have expressed themselves in these remains. Ask the right questions of this evidence and it will speak clearly of the ways in which men have lived, worked, played, worshiped, and died. It will even at times reveal how men thought and how they felt. An aesthetic sense may be detected in the form of a pot or its decoration; skill is at once apparent in the cutting of a design on a stamp seal of hard stone; business acumen is evidenced in the production and export of large quantities of wine; a concern for civil defense, which appears in an elaborately protected water system, points to the age-old problem of war and aggression; cultic objects speak of man's faith in powers beyond him and of his efforts to control them; and the provisions for the dead display a persistent belief in the life after death. Through such deductions as these the archaeologist arrives at a knowledge of how others have lived in the past. "The man who knows and dwells in history," said Sir Flinders Petrie, "adds a new dimension to his existence; he no longer lives in the one plane of present ways and thoughts, he lives in the whole space of life, past, present and dimly future."[2]

The window through which the archaeologist views the past is unique. While the literary sources that have been handed down to us frequently present unusual experiences of the kind that were considered important at the time, the record of man's daily life, often monotonous and deemed by him unworthy of recording, is to be read from the artifacts that he left. From this unpretentious testimony of what life was really like one gets an intimate view of the past.

Anyone who digs in what has come to be called the Holy Land is asked sooner or later the question, "Are you trying to prove that the Bible is true?" The Bible is, without doubt, the most important single monument left by the people of

[2] *Methods and Aims in Archaeology*, 1904, p. 193.

Palestine. Containing as it does literature written over a span of a thousand years, it is a unique witness to a faith held to tenaciously by the very people with whose history and culture the archaeologist is concerned. The Bible is primarily a book of faith. Yet it contains history. The historical details have been presented for the instruction of the readers and hearers in a faith that was the center of concern for the various writers and editors of the Bible. Obviously the methods of archaeological science can neither prove nor disprove the major themes of faith which the Bible asserts. Archaeology is able, however, to lay bare evidence that is useful in interpreting and evaluating the accounts of events narrated in the Bible. One who is concerned about learning what lies back of the formulation of the faith of biblical people is not disturbed to find that a certain biblical tradition lacks historical support, nor is he surprised to discover that the historical memory of the Bible is accurate.

Gibeon appears in the Bible as an important city and is the scene of well-remembered events. Fortunately we have been able to establish a bridge between these literary references and the actual remains found at el-Jib. Actual words in the Hebrew Bible correspond, letter for letter, to words excavated from the earth. No small part of the fascination that the work at el-Jib has held for us has been the interlacing of archaeological with biblical evidence. In the making of this tapestry of the history of the ancient city, the threads of evidence cannot be altered or tampered with. Where the evidence from one source does not fit that from another, one must conclude that the literary evidence has been distorted as it has been made to do service to some religious theme of the writer, or that the record has been altered in the process of transmission, or that the archaeological evidence is incomplete or incorrectly interpreted. In cases of conflict one can only record honestly what is found.

The satisfaction of having made a careful and objective record that can be placed at the disposal of future generations is a sufficient reward.

Actually, as we shall see, the results at el-Jib have in a remarkable degree been congenial to the literary accounts preserved in the Bible. In addition to these significant correspondences there have been discovered details about industry, commerce, and daily life which illuminate and supplement the written tradition.

CHAPTER II

THE LINK WITH THE BIBLE

Gibeon was a great city,
like one of the royal cities . . . and all its men
were mighty.—JOSH. 10:2

T H E first scientific explorer to leave anything like a descriptive account of the village of el-Jib and its antiquities was Edward Robinson. In 1838 this American scholar, competent in the field of biblical studies, made a visit of less than two and one-half months to Palestine and later published an account of his journey in *Biblical Researches in Palestine*, a work which laid the foundation for the modern science of Palestinology. Robinson spent exactly forty minutes at el-Jib on May 5, 1838. Yet on this hurried visit he observed enough about the place and its region to arrive at the conclusion that "el-Jib and its rocky eminence" was the ancient Gibeon of the Scriptures.

It is no wonder that Robinson did not stay longer at el-Jib. On the Saturday morning of his visit he and the six persons with him had pulled the stakes of their tent, which had been pitched for the night at Taiyebeh, and mounted their horses at 4:50 A.M. for the ride to Jerusalem. The night had not been a restful one. Robinson wrote of it in his diary: ". . . what with the voices of the Arabs, the barking of dogs, the crawling of fleas, and the hum of mosquitos, we were none of us able to get much sleep all night."[1]

[1] *Biblical Researches in Palestine*, 1874, vol. 1, p. 446.

As Robinson came upon the "beautiful" plain in which el-Jib is situated he was impressed by its fertility and by the natural protection that the rocky hill enjoyed. He described the hill on which el-Jib stood as "composed of horizontal layers of limestone rock, forming almost regular steps, rising out of the plain; in some parts steep and difficult of access, and capable of being everywhere very strongly fortified. . . . The hill may be said to stand in the midst of a basin, composed of broad valleys or plains, cultivated and full of grain, vineyards, and orchards of olive and fig trees. It was decidedly the finest part of Palestine, that I had yet seen."[2]

In a brief paragraph Robinson described what antiquities he saw at el-Jib in 1838. Everything that he listed can be seen by a visitor now, a century and a quarter later. Robinson wrote:

We reached the village of el-Jib situated on the summit of this hill at a quarter before 2 o'clock. It is of moderate size; but we did not learn the number of souls. The houses stand very irregularly and unevenly, sometimes almost one above another. They seem to be chiefly rooms in old massive ruins, which have fallen down in every direction. One large massive building still remains, perhaps a former castle or tower of strength. The lower rooms are vaulted, with round arches of hewn stones fitted together with great exactness. The stones outside are large; and the whole appearance is that of antiquity. Toward the east the ridge sinks a little; and here, a few rods from the village, just below the top of the ridge towards the north, is a fine fountain of water. It is in a cave excavated in and under the high rock, so as to form a

2 *ibid.*, pp. 454-455.

large subterranean reservoir. Not far below it, among the olive trees, are the remains of another open reservoir, about the size of that at Hebron; perhaps 120 feet in length by 100 feet in breadth. It was doubtless anciently intended to receive the superfluous waters of the cavern. At this time no stream was flowing from the latter.[3]

The building that Robinson guessed to have been a former castle with vaulted rooms is still standing today in the middle of the town and is used to shelter a villager's livestock; the fine fountain of water which he observed is the *ein el-beled*, the village spring; "the cave" under the high rock is the cistern room at the end of the tunnel which we cleared in 1956; and the open reservoir, which Robinson roughly estimated to measure 100 by 120 feet—it is actually 37 by 60 feet—is the reservoir in which we made a sounding during our first season of work.

Upon what did Robinson base his conclusion that this was the site of ancient Gibeon? The guiding principle of Robinson's researches was the hypothesis, which he was the first to utilize in locating biblical sites, that remnants of ancient place names hang on tenaciously, even when the older inhabitants are displaced by newer peoples with a different language. On the same two-day journey that included the hurried survey of el-Jib Robinson had applied his general principle to the names of no less than four other villages, where he saw a biblical name carried down faithfully in the present-day Arabic name for the place. Modern Anata he took to be Anathoth, the home of Jeremiah. He saw the ancient Geba in the present-day Jeba. In the sound of Mukhmas he could hear the echo of Michmash, the scene of the famous battle between Saul and the Philistines. The modern Beitin should correspond to the biblical Bethel,

[3] *ibid.*, p. 455.

where Jacob had his famous dream of angels ascending and descending the ladder.

Ancient names had been kept alive by the common people of Palestine with a tenacity that defied the efforts of Greek and Roman conquerors to change them. The native tradition about the proper name for a place was drawn in by the peasant with his mother's milk, Robinson argued. He put the principle of conservatism in the transmission of place names thus:

> The Hebrew names of places continued current in their Aramaean form long after the times of the New Testament; and maintained themselves in the mouths of the common people, in spite of the efforts made by Greeks and Romans to supplant them by others derived from their own tongues. After the Muhammedan conquest, when the Aramaean language gradually gave place to the kindred Arabic, the proper names of places, which the Greeks could never bend to their orthography, found here a ready entrance; and have thus lived on upon the lips of the Arabs, whether Christian or Muslim, townsmen or Bedawin, even unto our own day, almost in the same form in which they have also been transmitted to us in the Hebrew Scriptures.[4]

It was on the basis of this hypothesis that Robinson identified el-Jib with ancient Gibeon. The two consonants *jb* of Jib represented an abridged form of the four consonants in the Hebrew Gibeon (*gb'n*). Since there is no *g* in Arabic, the *j* is used to represent the sound in the ancient form of the name. Robinson admitted that he was troubled by the omission of the *ayn* (') of the Hebrew form of the name as it had passed over into Arabic. Yet he did not feel

[4] *ibid.*, p. 255.

that the difficulty was weighty enough to cause him to qualify his equation.

Another bit of evidence upon which this early explorer relied was the information that Flavius Josephus, the Jewish historian of the first century A.D., gives about the location of Gibeon, which in Greek appears as Gabaon or Gabao. In one place Josephus gives the distance from Gibeon to Jerusalem as 50 stadia (furlongs);[5] in another, the distance is given as 40 stadia.[6] This discrepancy suggests that both figures were merely conjectural estimates. Robinson estimated the shortest ancient route between el-Jib and Jerusalem, that which would have gone by Nebi Samwil, to have been about 60 stadia. The orientation of el-Jib from Jerusalem also fits the data given by Josephus about Gibeon in his *Jewish War*. There he describes the advance of Cestius in October of A.D. 66 from Lydda, through Bethhoron, to Gabao, "50 furlongs distant from Jerusalem."[7] Robinson was quick to observe that the present camel-road from Jaffa to Jerusalem passes to the north side of el-Jib, as anciently in like manner it passed by Gibeon. He also noted that the wealthy Roman matron Paula in her two-year pilgrimage, described by her friend and master Jerome in the fourth century, is said to have seen Gibeon on the right as she ascended the mountains at the two Beth-horons.[8]

It is noteworthy that this first scientific visitor to el-Jib was troubled by some contradictory evidence in an important ancient source and he did not hesitate to mention it. Eusebius, Bishop of Caesarea, in his famous geographical work of the third century called the *Onomasticon*, placed Gibeon four Roman miles to the west of Bethel.[9] Unfortu-

[5] *Jewish War*, ii, 516 (Loeb ed.).
[6] *Jewish Antiquities*, vii, 283 (Loeb ed.).
[7] *Jewish War*, ii, 516 (Loeb ed.).
[8] *Biblical Researches in Palestine*, 1874, vol. 1, p. 456.
[9] *ibid.*, vol. 1, p. 455.

nately there is no ruin which could possibly be a candidate
for the site of Gibeon at this distance to the west of Bethel.
Since el-Jib lies to the southwest of Bethel at a distance of
about seven Roman miles, measured in a straight line, it
can hardly meet the requirements of the location listed in
the *Onomasticon*. The information given by Eusebius is
further confounded by the text of Jerome's translation of
this geographical work, in which he locates Gibeon at the
same distance to the east of Bethel.

Robinson had been preceded by two travelers who had
written accounts of their visits to the vicinity of el-Jib and
who had ventured, without supporting argument, to asso-
ciate the site with Gibeon. Franz Ferdinand von Troilo, a
Silesian nobleman, who is said to have been well-meaning
but credulous, suggested the equation as a result of his
travels about the Holy Land in 1666.[10] In 1738, just a
century before Robinson's celebrated visit, Richard Pococke,
later Bishop of Meath, looked down upon el-Jib from Nebi
Samwil and supposed it to have been Gibeon.[11] Yet for these
two travelers, as for a long line of pilgrims, the locating of
ancient sites on the face of the land was merely the accept-
ance of a pious tradition and not the result of the application
of any scientific or historical method.

The events that have made the city of Gibeon of interest
are those that have been preserved in Israel's tradition.
Gibeon is the scene of many long-remembered and significant events mentioned in the Old Testament. Through its
gates and beside its copious waters there had passed,
through the six centuries of its recorded history, a long line
of colorful and well-known figures: Joshua, the conqueror;
Abner, the commander-in-chief of Saul; Joab, his counter-
part in the army of David; Zadok, David's priest; Amasa,
who was murdered there by Joab; Rizpah, Saul's wife;

[10] *ibid.*, vol. 1, p. 456.   [11] *ibid.*, vol. 1, p. 456.

seven sons of Saul; King Solomon; Hananiah, the false prophet who opposed Jeremiah; Ishmael, who slew the Judaean governor Gedaliah; and Johanan, the leader of the remnant of Judah, who took Jeremiah and other refugees into Egypt. This formidable list of heroes and villains is associated at one time or another with the city in the forty-five references in the Bible to it or to its people.[12]

Not only important people but significant events as well are associated with Gibeon in Israel's history, extending from the period of the conquest of Canaan to the Babylonian exile. The modern historian who seeks to make use of these colorful stories must remind himself that he is not dealing with archives nor with documents that were written down at the time of the events that are narrated. The biblical material that mentions the city of Gibeon has had a long literary history, and it may well have been transmitted by oral tradition for a considerable period of time before it was first written down.

Although these stories are contained in a book that is primarily concerned with religious faith and practice, they contain clues for the history of the city from the early days of the conquest by Joshua to the days when the land was laid waste by Nebuchadnezzar of Babylon. The episodes cluster around three major periods in the history of the nation: the conquest of Canaan; the monarchy of Saul, David, and Solomon; and the Babylonian exile. We shall consider the material preserved in the Old Testament for each of these periods.

The first picture in the Bible of Gibeon and its people is the account of how Joshua, the successful conqueror of the

---

[12] The name "Gibeon" (or "Gibeonite") appears in Josh. 9:3, 17; 10:1, 2, 4, 5, 6, 10, 12, 41; 11:19; 18:25; 21:17; II Sam. 2:12, 13, 16, 24; 3:30; 20:8; 21:1, 2, 2, 3, 4, 9; I Kings 3:4, 5; 9:2; I Chron. 8:29, 29; 9:35, 35; 12:4; 14:16; 16:39; 21:29; II Chron. 1:3, 13; Neh. 3:7, 7; 7:25; Isa. 28:21; Jer. 28:1; 41:12, 16.

well-fortified cities of Jericho and Ai, was deceived by the disguised Gibeonites into making a covenant of peace with them. The scene is preserved in Chapter 9 of Joshua:

> But when the inhabitants of Gibeon heard what Joshua had done to Jericho and Ai, they on their part acted with cunning, and went and made ready provisions, and took worn-out sacks upon their asses, and wineskins, worn-out and torn and mended, with worn-out, patched sandals on their feet, and worn-out clothes; and all their provisions were dry and moldy.
>
> And they went to Joshua in the camp at Gilgal, and said to him and to the men of Israel, "We have come from a far country; so now make a covenant with us."
>
> But the men of Israel said to the Hivites, "Perhaps you live among us; then how can we make a covenant with you?"
>
> They said to Joshua, "We are your servants."
>
> And Joshua said to them, "Who are you? And where do you come from?"
>
> They said to him, "From a very far country your servants have come, because of the name of the Lord your God; for we have heard a report of him, and all that he did in Egypt, and all that he did to the two kings of the Amorites who were beyond the Jordan, Sihon the king of Heshbon, and Og king of Bashan, who dwelt in Ashtaroth. And our elders and all the inhabitants of our country said to us, 'Take provisions in your hand for the journey, and go to meet them, and say to them, "We are your servants; come now, make a covenant with us."' Here is our bread; it was still warm when we took it from our houses as our food for the journey, on the day we set forth to come to you,

but now, behold, it is dry and moldy; these wineskins were new when we filled them, and behold, they are burst; and these garments and shoes of ours are worn out from the very long journey."

So the men partook of their provisions, and did not ask direction from the Lord. And Joshua made peace with them, and made a covenant with them, to let them live; and the leaders of the congregation swore to them. (Josh. 9:3-15)

After three days the Israelites learned the truth about these emissaries: they were not from a far country, but were Gibeonites from the Hivite enclave of the cities of Chephirah, Beeroth, and Kirjath-jearim, all of which lay within six miles of Gibeon (Text Fig. 3). Joshua remained true to his oath of the covenant that he had made with them, but he cursed the deceivers with the perpetual role of menial service; they were sentenced to become "the hewers of wood

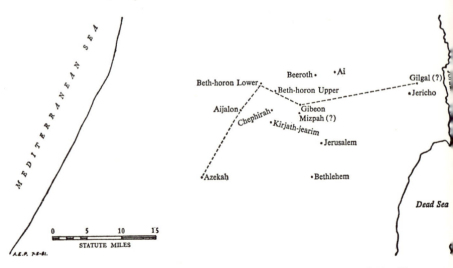

3. The route of Joshua's march from Gilgal to Gibeon to defend his allies. Joshua pursued the Amorite kings as far as Azekah.

and the drawers of water." Although the Gibeonites were
punished for their deception, for their belief that the command of the Lord to Israel to destroy all the inhabitants of
the land would be carried out they were rewarded by being
allowed to remain alive within their own city. Menial service
was indeed better than total extermination.

There is a sequel to this story of Joshua's covenant with
the Gibeonites. The king of Jerusalem, Adoni-zedek, was
alarmed by the news of the defection of the inhabitants of
Gibeon, whose city was said to have been "a great city, like
one of the royal cities," greater than Ai. Quickly he sum-
moned the aid of four kings of Amorite cities to the south
and together they laid siege to the fortified city of Gibeon.
The attack upon this city would serve, if successful, not
only to punish the Gibeonites for their collaboration with
the enemy, but also to strengthen the defense lines of the
hill country against the further penetration of the Israelites
into the territory of the Amorite city-states of Canaan.

The men of Gibeon made a second visit to Joshua at
Gilgal. This time they were not disguised, but they were
no less frightened than they had been on their first visit.
In response to their plea for speedy help, Joshua set out
with his army to fulfill his obligation to protect his ally,
with whom he had only recently entered into a covenant
(Text Fig. 3). The account of this battle between Joshua
and the five Amorite kings appears in Chapter 10 of Joshua:

So Joshua came upon them suddenly, having
marched up all night from Gilgal. And the Lord threw
them into a panic before Israel, who slew them with
a great slaughter at Gibeon, and chased them by the
way of the ascent of Beth-horon, and smote them as
far as Azekah and Makkedah. And as they fled before
Israel, while they were going down the ascent of Beth-

horon, the Lord threw down great stones from heaven
upon them as far as Azekah, and they died; there were
more who died because of the hailstones than the men
of Israel killed with the sword.

Then spoke Joshua to the Lord in the day when the
Lord gave the Amorites over to the men of Israel; and
he said in the sight of Israel,
"Sun, stand thou still at Gibeon,
and thou Moon in the valley of Aijalon."
And the sun stood still, and the moon stayed,
until the nation took vengeance on their enemies.
Is this not written in the Book of Jashar? The sun
stayed in the midst of heaven, and did not hasten to
go down for about a whole day. There has been no
day like it before or since, when the Lord hearkened
to the voice of a man; for the Lord fought for Israel.
(Josh. 10:9-14)

From these dramatic and obviously folk narratives it may
be deduced that at the time of the Israelite conquest Gibeon
was a large, fortified city, governed by elders, and allied
with three other cities in the immediate vicinity. This Hivite
(or Horite) league, as it was called, was opposed by a
formidable coalition of Amorite kings from the south who
attacked the principal Hivite city of Gibeon for the peace
that it had negotiated with the invaders.

There is, perhaps, an allusion to the religion of the
Gibeonites in the ancient couplet quoted in Joshua from the
lost Book of Jashar. Is it possible that the Sun-god was
worshiped at Gibeon and that the Moon-god was the patron
deity of the nearby Aijalon? If so, these specific locations
for the sun and moon, over Gibeon and the valley of Aijalon
respectively during the miraculously lengthened day and
night, are most appropriate.[13]

[13] J. Dus, *Vetus Testamentum*, vol. 10, 1960, pp. 353-374.

After appearing suddenly in Israel's history at the time of the conquest, Gibeon drops out of the picture for a period of almost two centuries. The city does not figure in the stories about the Judges, nor is it mentioned in the histories of Samuel and Saul in the Book of I Samuel. But during the reign of King David, in the first half of the tenth century, Gibeon is mentioned in connection with three incidents, each of which has a distinctly gruesome aspect.

The first of these episodes takes place soon after the death of Saul. Saul's son Ish-bosheth was seeking to maintain the throne of his father against the growing opposition of the talented and resourceful David. After Abner, Saul's commander-in-chief, had made Ish-bosheth king at Mahanaim in Transjordan, he brought servants of Ish-bosheth to Gibeon. There he met the doughty Joab, who had presumably come up from Hebron with a contingent of David's forces, at the "pool of Gibeon." The account of the celebrated contest at the pool is given in Chapter 2 of II Samuel:

And Joab the son of Zeruiah, and the servants of David, went out and met them at the pool of Gibeon; and they sat down, the one on the one side of the pool, and the other on the other side of the pool.

And Abner said to Joab, "Let the young men arise and play before us."

And Joab said, "Let them arise."

Then they arose and passed over by number, twelve for Benjamin and Ish-bosheth the son of Saul, and twelve of the servants of David. And each caught his opponent by the head, and thrust his sword in his opponent's side; so they fell down together. Therefore that place was called Helkath-hazzurim, which is at Gibeon. And the battle was very fierce that day; and Abner and the men of Israel were beaten before the servants of David. (II Sam. 2:13-17)

There ensued a larger battle in which Abner was beaten and forced to flee. Although the meaning of the puzzling name Helkath-hazzurim is not clear—it has been variously interpreted as "field of plotters," "field of liers-in-wait," "field of flints," "field of (sword-) edges," "field of sides," and "field of enemies"—this spot beside the "pool of Gibeon" long remained a landmark associated with the decisive contest that determined the succession to the throne of Israel.

Another incident of violence at Gibeon during the time of David is that of the murder of Amasa by Joab. As soon as David had dealt with the abortive attempt of his son Absalom to take his throne, he was faced with a revolt that was led by Sheba, a Benjaminite. Amasa was sent by David to call together the men of Judah within three days. Three days passed and Amasa did not appear. When Joab was sent on a mission to deal with a threat of rebellion in the north, the general apprehensions about the loyalty of the missing Amasa were found to be justified as Amasa was encountered with the enemy at Gibeon. The meeting of Joab with Amasa is described in Chapter 20 of II Samuel:

> When they were at the great stone which is in Gibeon, Amasa came to meet them. Now Joab was wearing a soldier's garment, and over it was a girdle with a sword in its sheath fastened upon his loins, and as he went forward it fell out.
>
> And Joab said to Amasa, "Is it well with you, my brother?" And Joab took Amasa by the beard with his right hand to kiss him. But Amasa did not observe the sword which was in Joab's hand: so Joab struck him with it in the body, and shed his bowels to the ground, without striking a second blow; and he died. . . . And Amasa lay wallowing in his blood in the highway.

And anyone who came by, seeing him, stopped; and when the man [one of Joab's men] saw that all the people stopped, he carried Amasa out of the highway into the field, and threw a garment over him. When he was taken out of the highway, all the people went on after Joab to pursue Sheba the son of Bichri. (II Sam. 20:8-10, 12-13)

Two specific details in this story are of some topographical importance. One is the mention of "the great stone which is in Gibeon," a possible reference to the stone of an altar at the high place of Gibeon, at which Solomon later sacrificed. The other detail of interest is the location of Gibeon on the main highway (*m^esillah*) leading from Jerusalem northward to the center of the tribe of Benjamin.

The third incident involving Gibeon and its inhabitants is the human sacrifice of seven descendants of Saul by the Gibeonites in order to terminate a three-year famine. Saul had slain the Gibeonites in violation of the solemn covenant which had been made between Israel and the men of Gibeon. Although there is no record elsewhere in the Old Testament of Saul's having put the Gibeonites to death, atonement for this breach of peace could only be made, so the Gibeonites assured David, by hanging two sons and five grandsons of the offending Saul "before the Lord at Gibeon." The shocking tale of human sacrifice and the picture of Rizpah, Saul's widow, watching over the corpses are given in Chapter 21 of II Samuel:

Now there was a famine in the days of David for three years, year after year; and David sought the face of the Lord.

And the Lord said, "There is blood guilt on Saul and on his house, because he put the Gibeonites to death."

So the king called the Gibeonites. Now the Gibeonites were not of the people of Israel, but of the remnant of the Amorites; although the people of Israel had sworn to spare them, Saul had sought to slay them in his zeal for the people of Israel and Judah. And David said to the Gibeonites, "What shall I do for you? And how shall I make expiation, that you may bless the heritage of the Lord?"

The Gibeonites said to him, "It is not a matter of silver or gold between us and Saul or his house; neither is it for us to put any man to death in Israel."

And he said, "What do you say that I shall do for you?"

They said to the king, "The man who consumed us and planned to destroy us, so that we should have no place in all the territory of Israel, let seven of his sons be given to us, so that we may hang them up before the Lord at Gibeon on the mountain of the Lord."

And the king said, "I will give them." . . .

The king took the two sons of Rizpah the daughter of Aiah, whom she bore to Saul, Armoni and Mephibosheth; and the five sons of Merob the daughter of Saul, whom she bore to Adriel the son of Barzillai the Meholathite; and he gave them into the hands of the Gibeonites, and they hanged them on the mountain before the Lord, and the seven of them perished together. They were put to death in the first days of harvest, at the beginning of barley harvest.

Then Rizpah the daughter of Aiah took sackcloth, and spread it for herself on the rock, from the beginning of harvest until rain fell upon them from the heavens; and she did not allow the birds of the air to come upon them by day, or the beasts of the field by night. (II Sam. 21:1-6, 8-10)

From this story it is apparent that as late as the time of David the people of Gibeon had not been fully assimilated into the body of Israel, since the Gibeonites did not assert the right of blood revenge for the men of their city whom Saul had put to death. Saul had been hostile to Gibeon, while David apparently was on good relations with the city and sought to remove the offense which his predecessor had given.

Where was the "mountain of the Lord" at Gibeon? It has been suggested that Nebi Samwil, the most conspicuous mountain in the vicinity of Gibeon and lying a mile to the south of el-Jib, may have been the site of the execution of the seven sons of Saul. It is thus not improbable that this neighboring high place was the location of Gibeon's sanctuary.

By the beginning of Solomon's reign, about 960 B.C., Gibeon, the former Hivite city, had become a part of Israel. The pagan associations connected with its high place had been forgotten or purified by an appropriate ritual. For it was to this ancient high place that Solomon went before the construction of the temple in Jerusalem to offer his impressive holocausts. The account in Chapter 3 of I Kings reads:

> And the king went to Gibeon to sacrifice there, for that was the great high place; Solomon used to offer a thousand burnt offerings upon that altar.
>
> At Gibeon the Lord appeared to Solomon in a dream by night; and God said, "Ask what I shall give you."
>
> And Solomon said . . . , "Give thy servant therefore an understanding mind to govern thy people, that I may discern between good and evil. . . ."
>
> It pleased the Lord that Solomon had asked this. And God said to him, "Because you have asked for this, and have not asked for yourself long life or riches

or the life of your enemies . . . behold, I give you a wise and discerning mind, so that none like you has been before you and none like you shall arise after you. I give you also what you have not asked, both riches and honor, so that no other king shall compare with you, all your days." (I Kings 3:4-6, 9-13)

The Chronicler adds to this tradition that Gibeon was also the place where the tent of meeting was (II Chron. 1:3, 13) and that the tabernacle and the altar of burnt offering were also a part of the cultic installation (I Chron. 16:39).

From the end of the tenth century, when it was a cult center for Israel in the early days of Solomon's reign, until the end of the seventh century, Gibeon is not mentioned in any historical writings of the Bible. It did not produce any prophet in the golden age of Israelite prophecy. The only prophet who is reported to have come from Gibeon is Hananiah, who, in the days of Nebuchadnezzar's pillaging of Jerusalem, prophesied that within two full years the Lord would break the yoke of Nebuchadnezzar from off all the nations. To this facile, optimistic prophet Jeremiah spoke the following harsh words:

Listen, Hananiah, the Lord has not sent you, and you have made this people trust in a lie. Therefore thus says the Lord: "Behold, I will remove you from the face of the earth. This very year you shall die, because you have uttered rebellion against the Lord." (Jer. 28:15-16)

The simple obituary of Hananiah follows this prediction of Jeremiah: "In that same year, in the seventh month, the prophet Hananiah died." (Jer. 28:17) Hananiah was indeed a prophet, but he brought no distinction to his city.

In the times of anarchy that followed the fall of Jerusalem in 586 B.C. Gibeon figures in the accounts of the

1. A view of el-Jib from Nebi Samwil as it appeared in an engraving of about two centuries ago.

2. El-Jib as it appears today from Nebi Samwil. The natural saddle-like hill rises to a height of approximately 200 feet above the surrounding plain.

3. The rich fields of the plain to the east of el-Jib
are cultivated by the villagers today as they were by
the Gibeonites, who lived on the southern part (left)
of the natural hill.

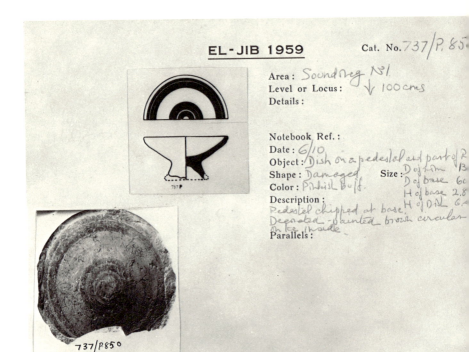

EL-JIB 1959   Cat. No. 737/P. 85

Area: *Sounding N1.*
Level or Locus: *↓ 100 cms*
Details:

Notebook Ref.:
Date: *6/10*
Object: *Dish on a pedestal and part of R*
Shape: *Damaged*   Size: *D of rim 13*
Color: *Pinkish Buff.*   *D of base 6c*
                        H of base 2.8
Description: *H of D NL 6.*
Pedestal chipped at base.
Decorated - painted brown circular
m ks inside
Parallels:

737/P85°

4. Catalogue card, made out in triplicate, giving information that will be used in the final publication.
A photograph of the dish is included and drawings of
its profile and the painted bands on the inside.

5. Abd Ibrahim Abdullah empties a basket of debris from the great pool upon the dump head.

6. The area immediately over the spring when excavations were begun there in 1956.

7. The area over the spring as it appeared at the close of the season. An arc of the rim of the great pool appears in the center.

8. Five-meter plots, laid out according to the grid, to the south of the pool. Stone walls to the right have been built during the course of the excavation to retain the debris.

9. The balk of every major cutting is carefully measured, and plotted by a draftsman. Tags on the balk indicate floor levels or other significant observations made during the course of excavation.

10. Ibrahim and Naji, two pottery washers, bending over the tub in which every piece of pottery is washed.

11. The pile of discarded pottery at the close of the 1956 season. Every sherd in this heap has been washed, sorted, and inspected by at least three people.

12. A storage jar of the Iron Age, crushed by the collapse of the roof of a house, has to be extracted carefully with trowel and brush.

13. Three Bronze Age vessels in place on the floor beside the wall of the room. After photography these were removed, cleaned, catalogued, and drawn to scale.

14. Joshua's slaughter of the Amorites at Gibeon.
Copy by Barruci of a part of the Joshua Roll now in
the Vatican. This eighth-century illustration of the
city of Gibeon shows the sun standing still at Joshua's
command.

15. Sheshonk's list of his conquests in Palestine, on
the wall of the Amon temple at Karnak, contains the
earliest surviving example (10th cent. B.C.) of the
name Gibeon (Fig. 16). The god Amon, with
sickle-sword in his right hand, leads by cords in
his left hand the bound captives, who are represented over the five rows of name-rings to the left of
the lower part of his figure. Gibeon is circled.

16. A drawing of a detail fro[m]
the list of Sheshonk at Karna[k]
showing Gibeon as bound captiv[e]

troubles that beset the small group of Judaean refugees, among whom was the prophet Jeremiah. When Ishmael had murdered the pro-Babylonian governor Gedaliah at Mizpah and had seized the Judaeans to take them captive to Ammon, he was met by the forces of Johanan at the "great waters that are in Gibeon" (so the Hebrew of Jer. 41:12). Ishmael's captives were taken away from him, but Ishmael himself escaped with eight of his men. From Gibeon the rescued "soldiers, women, children, and eunuchs" under the leadership of Johanan moved southward and took refuge near Bethlehem, fearful lest they be held responsible for the death of Gedaliah, whom the Babylonians had set over the land. These references tell us nothing about the condition of the city at the beginning of the exile. There is only the enigmatic reference to the "great waters," a phrase which could apply to the pool or to the spring of the village.

We are able to glean a little of the subsequent history of the city from the scattered references in Nehemiah and Chronicles. Men from Gibeon helped in the rebuilding of the wall of Jerusalem (Neh. 3:7); the people of Gibeon appear in a list of returning exiles (Neh. 7:25). In two places within I Chronicles there appears a genealogical list which links Gibeon with the house of Saul (8:29 and 9:35), and there is mentioned in this list a certain Gedor, a name containing the same three consonants which appear on jar handles found at el-Jib.

Although the Bible is the principal written source for the history of Gibeon, the city is mentioned elsewhere in ancient writings. The earliest of these extra-biblical references is the listing of the name Gibeon as one of the towns taken by the Egyptian king Sheshonk, or Shishak as he is called in the Bible. This king, who ruled from 945 to 924 B.C., invaded Palestine in the fifth year of the reign of King Rehoboam (I Kings 14:25) and returned home to erect a great display inscription on the south wall of the Amon temple at Karnak which listed the cities which he had taken (Fig. 15). The name Gibeon (*qb'n*) can be read there today neatly carved in hieroglyphs within an oval ring surmounted by the figure of a bound prisoner (Fig. 16). From this list of conquered towns it is possible to reconstruct the itinerary of Sheshonk and to determine what road the king took through central Palestine.[14] From Gaza Sheshonk moved up the seacoast and then turned inland to Gezer. From there he mounted the hills to Aijalon, Beth-horon, and Gibeon, which he claims to have taken. It is not impossible that the Egyptian king was at Gibeon when Rehoboam sent to him the tribute of the shields of gold which Solomon had made (I Kings 14:26) and by this payment saved his capital Jerusalem from attack.[15]

The Jewish historian Josephus, in his account of the attack of Cestius, the Roman governor of Syria, upon Jerusalem in A.D. 66, states that the Roman army camped at Gibeon after a march up the hill through Beth-horon.[16] After Cestius had failed in his attempt to take Jerusalem he returned to his former camping-place at Gibeon. Josephus describes the decision which Cestius made at Gibeon thus:

> Here Cestius halted for two days, uncertain what course to pursue; but, on the third, seeing the enemy's strength greatly increased and all the surrounding country swarming with Jews, he decided that the delay had been detrimental to him and, if further prolonged, would but increase the number of his foes. To accelerate the retreat, he gave orders to retrench all impedimenta. So the mules, asses, and all the beasts of burden were killed, excepting those that carried

[14] B. Mazar, *Vetus Testamentum*, Supplement IV, 1957, pp. 57-66.
[15] *ibid.*, p. 61.
[16] *Jewish War*, II, 515-516 (Loeb ed.).

missiles and engines of war; these they clung to for their own use, and, still more, from fear of their falling into Jewish hands and being employed against themselves. Cestius then led his army on down the road to Beth-horon.[17]

Cestius in his retreat down the pass at Beth-horon followed the same route which the Amorite kings took as they fled before Joshua and the forces of Israel.

We have seen how Edward Robinson studied carefully all these literary traditions about Gibeon—with the one exception of the Egyptian list of Sheshonk, which was not available to him in 1838—and how, with the topography of the region of el-Jib well in mind, he had concluded that the ancient Gibeon was to be equated with the modern el-Jib. It was as though he had solved a difficult jig-saw puzzle, making a complete picture out of many pieces. His conclusion as to where Gibeon should be located on the modern map was almost universally accepted by geographers, cartographers, and biblical historians for about a century.

Robinson's conclusion, however, was reexamined in 1926 by no less an authority than Professor Albrecht Alt, who has been called "the greatest biblical historian of his time."[18] Alt staunchly rejected the equation of Gibeon with el-Jib.[19] Gibeon should be located, he argued, at the modern Tell en-Nasbeh, a fine tell on the Jerusalem-Ramallah highway about four miles to the north of el-Jib. For this suggestion Alt made use of the one piece of evidence which Robinson had found to be recalcitrant, the statement of Eusebius in his *Onomasticon* that Gibeon lay four Roman miles west of

[17] *Jewish War*, II, 545-546 (Loeb ed.).
[18] W. F. Albright, *Journal of Biblical Literature*, vol. 75, 1956, p. 169.
[19] *Palästinajahrbuch*, vol. 22, 1926, pp. 11ff.

Bethel near Ramah. Since the third-century Bishop of Caesarea gave the distance in Roman miles, Alt maintained that Gibeon must have been situated on the Roman road, one which ran from Beitin through el-Bireh and beside Tell en-Nasbeh. Indeed the distance along this route is about four Roman miles; furthermore, Tell en-Nasbeh is near the modern er-Ram, the site of ancient Ramah.

But what important ancient city lay at el-Jib? There Alt placed the location of Beeroth, because of a remark in the *Onomasticon* that Beeroth was seven Roman miles from Jerusalem along the road to Nicopolis, the modern Amwas. There was nothing in the numerous biblical references which contradicted this new alignment for the locations of Gibeon and Beeroth, the two important cities of the Hivite league. The weight of the arguments of such a renowned authority as Professor Alt soon made itself felt and maps began to be published with Gibeon removed from el-Jib, where it had been confidently placed for almost a century.

The very same year that Alt published his identification of Gibeon with Tell en-Nasbeh, an American archaeologist, William F. Badè, decided to excavate the site. When the excavation had been completed and the results published in 1947 it became apparent that the link with ancient Gibeon was weak. The history of occupation at Tell en-Nasbeh did not fit the history of Gibeon as it is known from biblical sources. The city which stood at Tell en-Nasbeh had not been built until after the Late Bronze period, at the end of which Gibeon is said to have been a very great city.

In 1953 Alt again took up the question of the location of Gibeon.[20] He conceded that his suggestion, made a quarter of a century earlier, had been disproved by the results of excavation at Tell en-Nasbeh. Where then had Gibeon been situated? Alt suggested that the most likely spot was the

[20] *Zeitschrift des Deutschen Palästinavereins,* vol. 69, 1953, pp. 1ff.

modern village of el-Bireh, which is on the main road to the
north opposite the modern Ramallah. He cited the fact that
there was at el-Bireh a good spring at the southwest of the
village, which could correspond to the "great waters" mentioned in Jeremiah 41:12, and gave other reasons for
locating Gibeon here. He continued to identify el-Jib with
the ancient Beeroth. Professor Alt died in 1956, just two
months before the opening of the first excavation at el-Jib.

The evidence for the solution of this problem of the location of Gibeon turned up during our first season of work at
el-Jib. Suleiman, one of our pottery washers, was the first
to see the decisive evidence that terminated a long scholarly
controversy. As he sat at a wash tub brushing the dirt from
bits of pottery that had come from the great pool, he chanced
to notice some scratches on the upper side of a jar handle
(Fig. 17). Hopeful for *bakshish*, Suleiman handed the
fragment of handle to a member of the staff, who looked at
it for a few moments and then handed it to me.

"What does it say?" I asked skeptically, for not one of
the more than 50,000 pieces of broken pottery which had
been washed and scrubbed that season had an intelligible
letter on it.

"Gibeon," answered the supervisor facetiously.

We both laughed at the absurdity. The handle was
cleaned more carefully, placed in a paper bag and forgotten
until the evening, when it was again looked at under an
artificial light which could be slanted so as to cast shadows
across the cuttings on the handle. That evening it became
certain that the handle did indeed have upon it the four
Hebrew letters *gbʿn*, "Gibeon," the one word we most
wanted.

An archaeologist must be skeptical. Could this have been
a forgery? There were in Jerusalem some good friends
working on the Dead Sea scrolls, a half dozen people, any

one of whom knew exactly how to write the word Gibeon in archaic Hebrew script. Had one of them played a practical joke by scratching these four letters on a jar handle picked up on a visit to el-Jib and then "planted" it in a workman's basket? This suspicion was soon dispelled when we observed through a magnifying glass that across one of the strokes of the inscription there was a white line of limestone incrustation which must have taken a century or more to form. The inscription had been cut anciently; there could be no doubt about it.

A few days after this discovery another pottery washer, Ibrahim, upon returning from his lunch hour, took from his pocket another inscribed handle.

"I meant to show you this in the morning but forgot all about it until I found it in my pocket at lunch," he said with apologies.

Here in clean and neat script was *gbʻn-gdr*. There was no question about the authenticity of this "Gibeon" handle. It was a well-known type from the Iron Age and the writing had been done anciently in the style of the seventh or sixth century B.C. Soon there appeared a similar handle bearing the proper name Hananiah, a name which appears in Jeremiah 28:1, as the false prophet from Gibeon who opposed Jeremiah. Surely we had come upon the remains of a literate people.

To find in the ruins of a site the very name that scholars have long guessed to be that of the ancient city is something rare in the history of Palestinian archaeology. In the previous sixty-six years of scientific excavation it had happened only twice: James Starkey found during his fourth season at Tell ed-Duweir a potsherd on which there was written a communication in which the word Lachish appears; and the name Beth-shan was found in level V at Beisan within the text of a stela of Seti I. Yet in the first season of excavation at el-Jib two handles containing the name Gibeon had appeared.

Although the reading "Gibeon" was unmistakable, we were perplexed. Why should some ancient Israelite have gone to the trouble of scratching his name and his address on the handle of his jar? If it had been for the purpose of identifying his property then certainly the name of the owner would have sufficed. Civic pride could hardly have accounted for this practice. As long as the motive for the writing of the name of the city on the handle of a jar could not be explained satisfactorily there remained the disturbing possibility that these handles did not originate at el-Jib. Perhaps they had been carried anciently from a neighboring site, which was the true location of the biblical Gibeon.

The solution to this puzzle was not found until a year after the first discovery. In 1957, fifty-two more inscribed jar handles were discovered in the very same rock-cut pool which had produced the previous examples. Twenty-four of these bore the name Gibeon, spelled out in good archaic Hebrew (Figs. 18, 19, 20). This mass of evidence helped to remove the possibility of the jars having been imported from some other place.

In most cases "Gibeon" appears as a part of a formula. Following the place name is the puzzling word *gdr*, which in turn is followed by the name of a person. The most common is that of a certain Hananiah (son of) Nera. Here we have an immediate contact with the Bible. The name Hananiah appears frequently in the Old Testament and belongs to thirteen—or possibly fourteen—different persons, all of whom can be assigned to either Judah or Benjamin. In addition to Hananiah son of Azzur, from Gibeon, mentioned in Jeremiah 28:1, there is the perfumer who assisted in the repairing of the wall of Jerusalem and who stood next but one to a Gibeonite (Neh. 3:7-8). All of the twenty-seven occurrences of the name in the Bible are found in writings that can be shown to have been composed in the sixth century B.C. or later. To judge from the kind of letters employed on the handles from el-Jib it seems that this Hananiah Nera lived at the beginning of the period when the name Hananiah was popular, or only slightly earlier.

Another person named in the inscriptions is Azariah, a very common biblical name. There are no less than twenty Azariahs mentioned in the Bible. The most famous is the eighth-century king of Judah, who is mentioned by his name Uzziah in the famous vision of Isaiah in Chapter 6. Another Azariah is named as one of the Judaean children, who along with Daniel, refused the king's food and drink in Babylon (Dan. 1:6). With the appearance of this familiar biblical name at el-Jib we have another firm link between the results of archaeology and the ancient text of the Old Testament.

A third proper name which appears in the formula is Amariah. Like the other two this is a favorite name of biblical times, when it appears to have been used in the seventh-century book of Zephaniah and in the late books of Chronicles, Ezra, and Nehemiah. In addition to these three common biblical names there is the rare name Shebuel, which is mentioned in I Chronicles 26:24, and the unique Domla, a name which may mean something like "wait on the Lord."

In this small directory of the names of five citizens of Gibeon in the seventh-sixth century B.C. we have names which are either found in biblical writings or display formations consistent with elements that would have been quite natural in this period of Israel's history.

The most difficult problem in the formula is the word *gdr*, which whenever it appears follows the word Gibeon. There are two possibilities as to its meaning. If it is to be taken as a common noun, it must mean a "wall" or "fence," as it does in the Bible. In four biblical passages *gdr* is used for the wall of a vineyard. One of these is the story of Balaam and his ass in Num. 22:24-25, where it is associated with vineyards (*krmym*). These two verses read in a literal translation: "Then the angel of the Lord stood in the narrow way of the vineyards (*krmym*), an enclosure (*gdr*) on this side and an enclosure (*gdr*) on that side. And when the ass saw the angel of the Lord she pressed herself against the wall (*qyr*) and pressed the foot of Balaam against the wall (*qyr*); and he smote her again." From this text it would seem that *gdr* means something like the French *clos*, a section of the vineyards, a walled plot, possibly a property marked off by walls from neighboring properties. If this is the meaning of *gdr* on the handles, the formula could be translated thus: "Gibeon, the walled vineyard of Hananiah Nera / Azariah / Amariah."

There is yet another possibility. It is that *gdr* is a place name, Gedor. In I Chronicles 9:35-37 Gedor is mentioned along with Gibeon as the offspring of Jeiel. Since this passage seems to follow the practice of listing towns or districts by personal names from genealogies, the *gdr* of our formula could be interpreted as a place name in the Gibeon area. The two names would then signify the place Gibeon-Gedor.

What had the jars with inscribed handles been used for? Unfortunately no whole jars were found in the debris of the pool and no discernible residue could be detected on the fragments. However, from the best preserved examples of the jars it is possible to estimate the capacity as from 4 to 6 gallons. The relatively small mouth of the jar, measuring about 1½ inches in diameter, would have made it impracticable to place in it anything but a liquid, such as water, wine, or oil.

Two discoveries made in the same context which produced the inscribed handles provided some decisive clues. One was that of more than forty clay stoppers, which were found to fit neatly into the mouth of a jar (Figs. 21, 22). Although there were no string marks on the tops of these stoppers—they had been fired in a kiln before they had been used—it was obvious that a string placed through the two handles of the jar and over the top of the stopper would have held it firmly in place. The association of stoppers with remains of jars within the same deposit of debris in the pool and the correspondence in size between the beveled portion of the stoppers and the mouth of the jars make probable the conclusion that the stoppers had been made expressly for these very containers. If this supposition is right, then the liquid for which the jars were intended was not water, which would have warranted no such sealing. Obviously the liquid was either oil or wine, both of them relatively costly. The stoppers would have made it possible to transport the commodity a considerable distance. The decision as to which of the two products was shipped in the jars must be left until we consider the evidence found around the great pool from which the jar fragments came.

Another discovery is of considerable importance for settling the problem of the location of Gibeon. In the light of the evidence thus far produced, it is possible to maintain that the appearance of Gibeon on the handles at el-Jib is, in fact, strong evidence that Gibeon is to be located elsewhere. The site at el-Jib could well have been the destination for the jars which had been sent there from Gibeon. And what we have in the debris of the pool could thus have been the dump heap which contained the empty containers of wine or oil which had been exported from a distant Gibeon and consumed at this, another city.

A significant discovery, also from the same debris, served

to exclude this possibility. A clay funnel was found, made of the same type of clay and fired to the same color as one of the jars. When the funnel was placed in the mouth of the jar it was found to fit perfectly (Fig. 23). Certainly it had been made by the potter expressly for filling jars such as these, and most probably it had been made by the same potter who turned the containers. This bit of evidence strongly suggests that el-Jib was the place where the jars were filled with the liquid and not the destination at which they were emptied. The export from Gibeon of some relatively costly liquid seems to be established when one takes into account the entire evidence of the labels on the handles, the size of the mouth of the jar, the stoppers and the funnel.

What was the purpose served by the labels, giving the point of origin for the product which was exported and the names of the makers? There are two possibilities. The inscription may have been intended to assure the consumer in another town of the quality of the product. This explanation assumes, of course, that Gibeon enjoyed a reputation for its fine oil or wine and that the names of Hananiah Nera, Azariah, Amariah, Domla, and Shebuel were sufficiently well known to have had some commercial value in the surrounding districts where the product was marketed.

Another possibility is that the address and the name were written on the jars to facilitate the return of the containers when the contents had been consumed. The jars were probably of considerable value. If this is the correct explanation, then only the contents of the jar was sold and the jar itself was eventually returned to its proper owner at Gibeon for a refund or for a credit. The theory that the inscriptions were means for identifying returnable containers seems to be the more tenable one.

When we finished cleaning the pool in 1957 we had found sufficient evidence to settle the long debate over the location of biblical Gibeon. Gibeon was at el-Jib in biblical times. Robinson's guess had been proved correct. Our curiosity as to what the industry was which produced a product so widely exported could be satisfied only by the excavation of the areas around the pool in which this tantalizing material has been found. Thus at the end of the 1957 season the surrounding area was marked as the target for the next campaign. Two years later we attacked this area and found the answer to the puzzling question of what had been placed in the jars.

CHAPTER III

DRAWERS OF WATER

But Joshua made them that day hewers of wood and
drawers of water.—JOSH. 9:27

T H E most conspicuous physical feature of Gibeon, as it
is known from ancient sources, is its adequate supply of
water. The "great waters that are in Gibeon" made it a
choice camp site for the refugees after the catastrophe of the
destruction of Jerusalem by Nebuchadnezzar in 586 B.C.
The celebrated "pool of Gibeon" remained in Israel's historical memory as a landmark associated with a decisive
contest in David's struggle for the throne after the death of
Saul. Cestius made his camp there in A.D. 66, quite possibly
because of the availability of a good supply of water for
his soldiers and pack animals. In addition to specific references to water and to a pool there is the ancient tradition
that the Gibeonites had been condemned for their deception
of Joshua to become "drawers of water." This tradition may
have been strengthened by the common knowledge that
Gibeon had an abundant supply of water.

With such a tradition in the record from the past, it is
no surprise to find today a constant supply of running
water. One spring flows throughout the year from the base
of the hill; and seven smaller ones supplement the flow from
this major source. The Gibeonites took costly measures to
protect and to preserve this valuable natural resource. In
our first two seasons of work at el-Jib we found an impressive total of 172 steps, which in biblical times had been

chiseled from the solid rock of the hill to facilitate the labor
of the "drawers of water" as they made use of two elaborate
systems for delivering fresh water to those who lived within
the city's defenses.

When we began excavations at el-Jib in 1956 one of our
principal objectives was the exploration of a partly opened
tunnel that led into the rock of the hill at the point on the
east side from which issues the spring of the village.
Robinson had noted, on the occasion of his short but epoch-
making visit to el-Jib in 1838, that there was "a cave excavated in and under the high rock" near the spring, but he
had apparently not entered the cave, since he made no
mention of the stepped tunnel that connects with it. The
cave was entered, however, in the 1870's, when the Survey
of Western Palestine was made by Conder and Kitchener,
and the passageway leading off from the back was noted in
their report. Unfortunately it was impossible for these sur-
veyors to enter the tunnel that led from the cave because of
a stone wall that blocked the entrance.

In 1889 the rock-cut tunnel at the back of the cave was
entered and its lower course was measured by a Russian
who is known only by the name of "Mr. Risky." A plan and
a section of as much of the installation as the Russian could
actually explore were published the following year by Baurath C. Schick, a well-known German resident of Jerusalem,
in the *Quarterly Statement of the Palestine Exploration
Fund.*

When we began work at el-Jib we had this sketch that
Schick had published and a later, more accurate one made
by F. M. Abel in 1911, which had been published by H.
Vincent in his *Jérusalem antique.* These were good preliminary guides but neither, of course, followed the course
of the stepped tunnel under the city wall and into the city

since tons of debris clogged the upper reaches of the passageway.

The choice of a spot in which to begin to dig at a virgin site is an important decision. El-Jib presented an expanse of about sixteen acres of buried ruins, to judge from pottery which had washed out or had been plowed up by farmers. At best, we could hope to excavate carefully only a small fraction of this area during the first season of work.

We decided that the first area for attack should be a plot of farm land which lay on the very top of the hill immediately over the spring of the village (Fig. 6). There were two reasons for this choice. The tunnel, the lower end of which had long been known, should open into the city somewhere in this area. Since the opening to the tunnel would certainly be inside the city wall, a segment of the defensive system of the city should be along the rim of the hill immediately over the spring. Another reason for beginning the excavation in this spot was the probability of finding here good stratification of the various periods of human occupation at the site. Since the area above the spring enjoyed the natural protection of the rocky scarp of the hill and a ready access to the principal water supply, it was a likely place for houses at any period in the city's history. Thus, a cut here should give a profile of periods of occupation.

The choice was a lucky one. The city wall was encountered after only three days of work. Then, only a few days after this fortunate discovery a pickman raised his pick from the ground to see a small hole which he had accidentally cut into an underground chamber. I tried to sound the depth of the opening with a six-foot steel tape, but it would not reach bottom. We tied a nail to a cord and let it down for about 15 feet until it finally struck bottom. A larger opening was made and an adventuresome and excited workman, with a rope tied around his waist, was lowered by his fellows into the darkness below. We had been fortunate enough to find the roof to the upper section of the tunnel that connected the inside of the ancient city with the spring at the base of the hill. As we crowded around the edge of this man-hole the first explorer of the tunnel groped his way along its course and shouted up in Arabic his description of this important discovery.

Cleaning the tunnel of the tons of silt that had washed into it through the centuries from the opening at the top required over a month of work by as many workmen as we could possibly squeeze into the limited working space. The most difficult part of the tunnel was finally opened by the ingenuity of our foreman Abu Yusuf, who found that school-boys were best suited, both physically and temperamentally, to this task. By the use of songs to break the monotony and a system of rest periods, the boys were induced by the patient Abu Yusuf to stay at the job until the last basket of dirt was carried out of this dark tunnel and deposited outside.

The tunnel had been cut as a means for civil defense. The massive city wall which was built around the edge of the rocky scarp of the hill provided, when the city gates were shut and barred, an almost perfect defense against enemies on the outside (Text Fig. 4). Yet it had one weakness. The same wall that kept the enemy without the city served to separate the Gibeonites from their principal water supply, lying as it did outside the wall at the base of the hill. The wall could have been enlarged to encircle the area of the spring, but the natural defense provided by the high rocky scarp of the hill would have been sacrificed by the abandon-ment of the natural line of the wall.

A solution for this weakness in the defensive system was found by the ancient city planners (Text Fig. 5). A cave

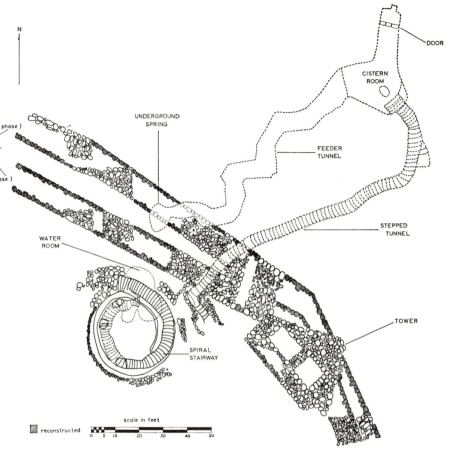

N

phase)

se)

UNDERGROUND
SPRING

WATER
ROOM

SPIRAL
STAIRWAY

scale in feet

reconstructed

0 5 10   20   30   40   50

DOOR

CISTERN
ROOM

FEEDER
TUNNEL

STEPPED
TUNNEL

TOWER

4. Plan of Gibeon's city wall and its two protected water systems.
The inner phase of the city wall is the older.

was hewn from the rock where the spring issued from the
base of the hill. A stone door at the entrance could keep an
enemy from the spring water that flowed into a basin
within the cave. At the back of the cave a tunnel was cut
through the solid rock of the hill on which the city stood
until it opened into the public square of the walled city. By

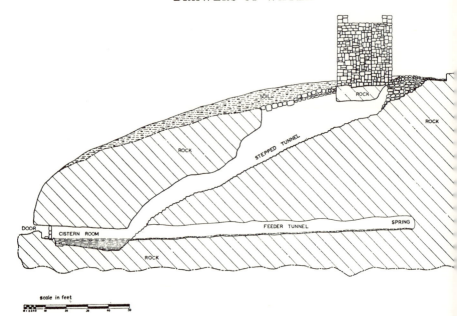

5. Section of the eastern side of the hill through which the stepped tunnel was cut to p[...] access to the spring from inside the city wall. The height of the wall is conjectural.

means of this tunnel the inhabitants of the city could have protected access to the fresh water lying 80 feet below their streets whenever they were under siege. The Gibeonites could withstand a siege almost indefinitely, provided they had their bins well stocked with food.

The effectiveness of this system of civil defense for withstanding sieges is attested by the fact that thus far in four campaigns of excavation we have found no evidence that the city was ever burned completely during the biblical periods of its history.

As one enters the cave, or cistern room, from the plain outside he sees two vertical grooves notched into the sides of the wall just inside the doorway and a corresponding groove in the floor (Fig. 28). These were obviously the slots into which a stone barricade, 30 inches thick, was erected to keep the attackers from the vital water supply of the city. The stones which had once served to form this precursor of a portcullis had long since been carried off, but there is no doubt as to the function of the cuttings in the sides and floor of the entranceway.

In times of peace the doorway from the cistern room to the plain outside was probably left open. Men who worked the fields around the city would have found this access to the water room more convenient than that of climbing up to the city and then down again through the tunnel to get water for themselves and for their animals. The door was probably so fashioned that it could be erected quickly in time of danger and then taken down when the crisis had passed. It is likely that large, well-hewn slabs were kept ready at hand so that they could be fitted into the grooves at the first alarm of the enemy's approach.

The cistern room extends into the hill for a distance of 39 feet and is approximately 10 feet high at the back (Fig. 29). A niche appears in the wall of the room. It had been cut obviously to hold a lamp which provided light for the water carriers when the chamber was closed to the outside.

From the southwest side of the cistern room a horizontal, or feeder tunnel has been cut to the spring, some 112 feet deep within the rock of the hill (Fig. 30). The winding course of this tunnel, which slopes slightly from the spring, suggests that the original excavators in their work merely followed the source of the water as it issued from the crevices. Their purpose was obviously that of increasing its flow by providing a better channel from the source to the cistern room. A channel had been cut in the floor of the tunnel to conduct the flow when it was smaller, as it always is in summer. At the spring itself the water flows evenly from small crevices in the rock floor.

The stepped tunnel which leads from the cistern room upward into the walled city follows a winding course over a distance, measured on the horizontal, of 148 feet. It would have been much shorter to bore in a straight line, but the engineers of this project probably followed a less direct course in order to take advantage of natural fissures in the rock to make the cutting easier.

As one begins to ascend the stairway of ninety-three steps, he first climbs seven steps with extremely narrow treads (Fig. 29). Most of these were probably covered over by the water in the cistern room. It may have been that they were cut purposely with narrow treads so that the water carriers could dip water from the pool of the cistern room without the danger of breaking a partly submerged vessel against the step below the surface.

Upon entering the opening to the tunnel itself one passes through a comparatively small, round opening. The water carrier could support himself against the sides of this doorway and thus reduce the possibility of slipping on a step which usually must have been wet with spilled water. After ascending nineteen more precipitous steps one comes to a sharp right turn. From this elbow the tunnel continues in a relatively straight direction until it reaches a point within a few steps from the opening into the city just inside the city wall.

We are able to determine how the main and longest segment of the tunnel was cut. Work was begun from the ground level. A deep trench was made in the limestone of the hill, extending from a point outside the city wall for a distance of 36 feet. When this gash in the rock had been cut to a depth of 14 feet one tunnel was bored in the general direction of the cistern room and another at the other end of the trench, under the city wall until it emerged within the city. When the tunneling was complete the open trench was roofed over. Stones were placed along each side of the cutting so that they projected slightly beyond the edge (Fig. 25). On top of these were placed huge slabs which spanned the remainder of the distance to form a stepped ceiling for the structure. This corbel served as a kind of primitive arch for the roof of the tunnel. A layer of dirt was placed over the roof to camouflage it. No enemy would ever suspect that beneath this innocent looking soil there was a secret passageway to fresh water by which the Gibeonites could keep themselves alive throughout a protracted siege.

The central segment of the tunnel is impressive as one looks down its long, narrow, Gothic-like passageway (Fig. 26). When we were excavating on this part of the mound in 1956, the freshly cleaned tunnel served as a cool and pleasant place in which to eat lunch. It was also reassuring to know that such a secure bomb shelter was always available as a refuge from the shells that were being fired during that season on the nearby Jordanian-Israeli border.

Throughout the entire course of the main segment of the tunnel there are lamp niches cut in the walls at regular intervals. Here oil lamps with flax wicks had been placed to provide light for the water carriers as they made their ways up and down the tunnel. Over one niche was a deposit of carbon from the olive oil that had burned in a lamp more than 2,500 years ago.

When we had completely cleaned the tunnel we were faced with the problem of getting light for photographing the dark recesses of this underground structure. Multiple flash units or powerful strobes, which the job required, were not to be had in Jerusalem. We finally solved the problem by coating boards with aluminum foil and flashing in the sunlight from outside by several relays of reflectors.

The sun had to be caught at just the hour when the shaft of sunlight through the opening we had made in the corbeled roof fell vertically into the tunnel. All of our photography had to be done in haste within a period of twenty minutes shortly after noon, as directions were shouted in Arabic to a series of assistants who held the aluminum reflectors.

The tunnel had been used over a very long period of time—how long it was impossible to determine. The treads of the steps exhibit a great deal of wear, particularly in the middle of the step where the traffic was heaviest (Fig. 27). Another evidence of extensive use of the passageway was discovered quite by accident. As staff members made use of this convenient passageway in moving from the excavation on top of the hill to another area which was being dug in the plain below the city, they frequently braced their hurried descent by placing their hands against the walls of the tunnel. In doing so they noticed that the surface of the walls at waist level was polished quite smooth in contrast to the rough pick-marked surface above and below. Apparently the carriers of water at Gibeon had braced themselves in exactly the same way when they had descended the steps and this daily use through centuries had worn a smooth band which extends from the top to the bottom of the tunnel on both sides.

When was this tunnel cut? It is obvious that the construction has no meaning as a defensive measure, which it obviously was, apart from its connection with the city wall which made secure its upper entrance. It must, therefore, have been constructed either at the time of the building of the wall or sometime after its completion. The upper end of the trenched and roofed portion of the tunnel extends to a point which is immediately below the exterior face of the outer phase of the massive city wall. Thus it is clear that this part of the city wall was standing at the time that the tunnel was cut. How old then is the city wall? Although further excavations along other segments of the long city wall may change the estimate, at the present stage of our knowledge it seems that the building of the city wall was not earlier than the beginning of the Iron Age, or about 1200 B.C. Furthermore, there are strong indications that the outer phase of the city wall, under which the builders of this water system were forced to tunnel rather than to make use of the easier method of trenching from the top, was an addition that was built to strengthen the original wall built a century or two earlier. Thus the cutting of the tunnel may be placed tentatively at about the time of the Hebrew Monarchy, or at about the tenth century B.C.

The hewing of the tunnel from relatively hard limestone with bronze or iron picks was a task which involved the expenditure of a great amount of labor. That this project of hydraulic engineering was carried through successfully either evidences a high degree of voluntary cooperation on the part of those who lived within the city, or suggests that there was a strong ruler who could impound labor for this important project.

Where did the Gibeonites get the idea of this ingenious device for withstanding a long siege? The nearest example of a similar water system is the stepped tunnel at Gezer, which lies 16 miles from Gibeon. The water table of this walled city lay 94 feet below the rock on which Gezer was built. To reach this water supply from within the city wall, a stepped tunnel was hewn from the rock at an angle of 39° for a total distance of 174 feet. Since this water source was within the hill itself, no barricade for protecting it from attackers was required. It is impossible to determine when the people of Gezer cut this tunnel.

An analogous defensive system for providing water from

a spring has appeared at Megiddo, where the excavators have been able to date the construction to the middle of the twelfth century B.C. Megiddo, like Gibeon, had a copious spring at the base of the hill on which the city stood at a height of 72 feet above the level of the spring. Yet the engineers at Megiddo solved the problem of access to the water differently. They first cut a vertical shaft equipped with steps into the rock of the hill to a depth slightly below the level of the spring on the side of the hill. They then connected the bottom of this stairway with the spring, which is 213 feet distant, by means of a horizontal tunnel. The water was channeled through this tunnel from the spring to the foot of the stairs, where it was readily available to the water carriers from within the city wall. A permanent wall was constructed to protect the spring from the outside.

What appears to be an exact parallel to the Gibeon tunnel is the ruin of a badly clogged tunnel at ancient Ibleam, located at the modern Khirbet Bel'ameh, just south of Jennin in Jordan. The stepped tunnel can be followed from the spring to a point about 98 feet within the hill, beyond which it is completely blocked with rubble. This installation, like the one at Gibeon, is fitted with lamp niches carved into the sides of the passageway. When Ibleam is excavated, it may well provide the most complete parallel to the tunnel at Gibeon.

In addition to these parallels from Palestine itself there are similar construction at Mycenae and Athens in Greece, and a stairway of 120 steps at Susa in Persia. In the light of the wide diffusion of this type of a protected water supply it is possible that the plan at Gibeon was not entirely original but was a cultural borrowing of a well-established and widely used device.

The most spectacular monument discovered in four seasons at el-Jib is the large pool with a spiral staircase, hewn from the bedrock of the hill just inside the wall on the north-east side of the city (Text Fig. 4). The cutting of this landmark of ancient Gibeon involved the quarrying and removal of approximately 3,000 tons of limestone, much of which was undoubtedly used in the construction or the re-building of the city wall which runs beside it. How long it must have taken to carve out this hole, 80 feet deep, cannot even be guessed with any degree of accuracy. It took the better part of two campaigns for as many men as could be conveniently put to work in the area to loosen and remove the dirt from this cutting. When one considers the hardness of the limestone which had to be quarried and picked with primitive metal tools, the feat of the pool's construction is a truly impressive one. Even with slave labor and hard task-masters the project must have required years to complete.

The discovery of the pool, unlike that of the tunnel, was a complete surprise. When we went to el-Jib for the first season of excavation, this ancient monument was filled in completely and further camouflaged with 3 or 4 feet of soil, on which the owner of the land was growing a luxuriant crop of tomatoes. The dramatic appearance of this pool underneath was as much of a surprise to the oldest villagers in el-Jib as it was to us.

When the gigantic proportions of this cutting in the rock began to become evident, a proud and imaginative citizen of the village told us that there was an ancient book which described the pool. When he was asked to go at once to the village and fetch the book—and the search was to be on our time and not the workman's—he returned shortly with a sheepish smile and the announcement that the book had been lost. From the nature and date of the debris which covered the rim of the pool we were certain that no one had seen even the outline of the upper part of this ancient construction for at least sixty generations.

The rim of the pool made its appearance about the middle of the first season (Fig. 7). At the time we thought that it was possibly a shallow basin cut into the rock for a depth of a few feet. We marked off a segment of it to be dug as a trench to find its depth. By the last day of that campaign we had dug the southern third of the pool to a depth of 35 feet without finding the bottom and had laid bare forty-two rock-cut steps of a stairway that spiraled around its wall. So narrow had our tapering trench become as we had dug it to a depth of 35 feet that it was impossible to go deeper without starting all over again from the top and making the trench larger. We left el-Jib that year excited, to be sure, by this impressive discovery but nevertheless haunted by the possibility that, had we been able to dig even inches deeper, we might have found the bottom.

The following season we went to el-Jib with the single objective of tidying up this one discovery. We began again at the top of the larger, remaining segment of the fill and with patience pushed our way down, this time cleaning the entire area of the pool as we went. Since it was possible to make use of only about forty workmen at one time in the restricted area of the pool, we decided to introduce shift work into the methods of archaeology. The summer days are long and we took advantage of every minute of light. Two gangs of laborers were employed. One shift of forty men began at 5:00 A.M., when the sun came up, and worked, with only a half hour's break for breakfast, until noon. A second group arrived at noon and literally took the tools from the hands of the first shift. They worked through, with only a fifteen minute break, until 6:30 P.M., when it became too dark to see and identify important objects which were imbedded in the debris. Fred V. Winnett supervised one shift for a week, while I took the other. Each week we alternated in taking the early assignment. By utilizing every minute of daylight over a six-week period we were able to accomplish what, by following regular working hours, would have taken twelve weeks. Each day we recorded our progress as we inched our way down. At the end of the season we found that we had averaged 2 feet and 5 inches a day.

The mechanics of removing the tons of dirt and stones from the pool presented a problem. Since there were no powered derricks or hoists in Jordan we began by using laborers to carry the debris up the anciently cut steps in sturdy baskets made from discarded automobile tires. This procedure was slow and seemed inefficient. We presented the problem to Professor Joe W. Kelly, of the Engineering Department of the University of California, who hastened to suggest the use of power-driven chains of buckets and other modern devices. When he learned that these were not available in Jordan he suggested the simple device of a wooden A-frame, two pieces of wood joined together at the top where a pulley could be attached for the rope by which the buckets of debris could be hoisted to the top of the pool. This seemingly excellent idea was tried early in the 1957 season (Fig. 32). But a brief trial of modern efficiency methods made it quite evident that our village laborers were not yet ready for mechanization. The operator at the top would occasionally let drop a 50-pound basket of rocks and dirt upon his helper 33 feet below—and all in good sport. If the helper remained unscathed, he would rush up the steps and engage his opponent, who protested that it had been only an accident, in a fist-to-fist encounter. American efficiency methods were soon abandoned as unrealistic. Laborers were deployed along the steps and up to the dump head to form a bucket line, and baskets of debris were handed from one man to another until they reached the top and were emptied (Fig. 31). Thus, after the expenditure of something like 23,000 weary man-hours, the bottom was finally reached at the end of August in 1957.

The monotony of the job was occasionally broken by contagious interest on the part of workmen as the pool became more and more impressive in size. Someone suggested that at the bottom there were the bodies of seven kings, each buried with his spear, and this grim picture of a royal past began to be passed around. This picture of what lay at the bottom of the pool never materialized, but it and others like it fabricated by workmen served to boost morale through some long, hot, and tiresome days.

It was only when we had cleared the pool to the bottom that it became apparent that the pool and stairway, like the stepped tunnel, had been cut to provide an access to the water available deep within the hill without exposing the water carriers to the hazards of the attack by an enemy outside the walls. It was another measure for civil defense. The project of cutting this stairwell had been begun ambitiously. A cylindrical shaft, measuring 37 feet in diameter, had been hewn from the rock to a depth of 35 feet (Fig. 34). In the cutting of the perpendicular sides of this cylinder there had been left a spiral stairway, 5 feet wide, beginning at the north side and winding downward around the edge of the pool in an easterly direction. The stairway was protected by a balustrade of live rock, slightly more than a foot and a half thick, which had been left at the outer end of the steps for the safety of the water carriers (Fig. 35).

When the cylindrical pool had been cut to a depth of 35 feet the stairway was continued below the floor level of the pool into a tunnel which followed the curving line of the rim above. Finally at a depth of 45 feet below the floor of the pool this stepped tunnel opens into a kidney-shaped water chamber (Fig. 36), measuring approximately 23 by 11

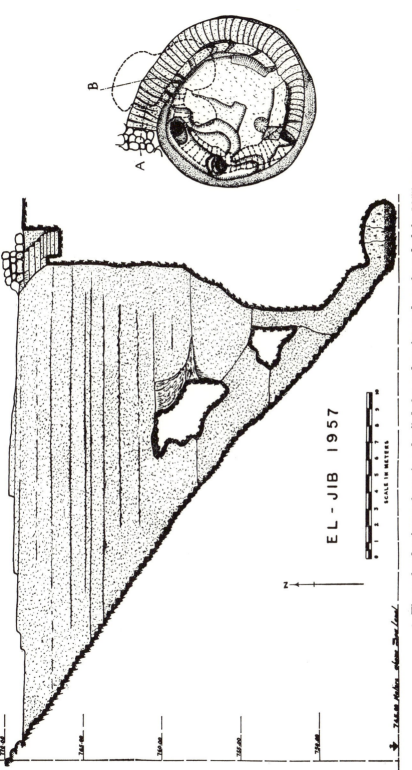

6. The pool-and-stairway shown in a detailed plan and section made at the end of the 1957 season.

EL - JIB 1957

SCALE IN METERS
0 1 2 3 4 5 6 7 8 9 10

N

feet. Here at the same level as that of the spring of the village, which had been tapped by the other stepped tunnel, fresh water appears. When our workmen made the break-through into the water chamber in 1957, an adventurous laborer crawled through the opening, tasted the water, and emerged triumphantly with the news that the water was good.

The stepped tunnel which led down to the water chamber was provided with light through two shafts which had been cut through the rock to the floor of the cylindrical pool, which was open to the sky. These openings supplied light for the water carriers who made use of this corkscrew-like tunnel on their descent to the water, which lies 80 feet below the solid rock of the city square above.

Lying in the fresh water of the underground reservoir were two jars that had obviously been abandoned by the last users of this water system. To judge from their form and shape they could not have been made later than the first part of the sixth century B.C., or the last days of the Judaean state. If a water carrier had heard word shouted from above that the city wall had been breeched and that the enemy was within the gates, he would certainly have abandoned his jar in the water chamber and have fled up the seventy-nine steps in search of safety. Perhaps the two Gibeonites had done just this. The mute evidence of the two abandoned jars was sealed up when the conqueror closed the tunnel leading to the water with huge blocks of limestone pried loose from the city wall and pushed over the side of the pool to choke for 2,600 years the spring that had en-abled the city to withstand siege as long as it did.

At the end of the first season we had thought that the pool was a reservoir intended to contain water. The sub-sequent discovery of the water chamber at the bottom made it clear, however, that it was but a part of a stairwell by which the drawers of water might have a convenient and safe access to the artesian source lying under the city.

Who was the conqueror who filled in this water source? A likely candidate is the Babylonian King Nebuchadnezzar, who is known from the Bible to have made two campaigns against the Judaean kingdom. One was in 598 B.C., when he carried King Jehoiachin into exile; the other was in 586 B.C., when Jerusalem was destroyed. Yet the evidence is not decisive, and the possibility that the pool was at least partly filled in as early as the end of the eighth century must not be excluded. In the year 701 B.C. the Assyrian King Sennacherib made a campaign to Palestine and later boasted in his inscriptions that he had conquered forty-six walled cities belonging to King Hezekiah of Judah. It is not impossible that Gibeon was one of the conquests of Sennacherib.

The date for the cutting of the pool is even more difficult to establish than that of its disuse. Yet there are some clues. Since it was a defensive measure it must have been cut after the building of the inner and earlier phase of the city wall which runs to the east of it. This fortification has been dated tentatively to the early part of the Iron I Age, i.e., the twelfth-eleventh centuries. The pool was constructed before the stepped tunnel leading to the spring, since the engineers of the latter had been forced to change the course of the tunnel at the upper end so that the entrance would not be at the very edge of the pool. A glance at the plans of the tunnel and the pool will reveal that the upper course of the tunnel makes a sharp 90° turn to the left so as to emerge from the rock at a safe distance from the edge of the pool. Obviously the pool was in existence when the tunnel was made. If the tunnel is to be dated to around the tenth century, as we have suggested above, then the construction of the pool may be placed somewhere within the twelfth and the eleventh centuries.

It seems highly probable that this expensive effort to supply the city with water by cutting through 80 feet of hard limestone to the water table of the hill was relatively unsuccessful. When we cleaned the steps of the stairs their edges were found to be sharp and straight, as though they had had little use. Compared to the well-worn steps of the tunnel to the spring at the base of the hill, these steps appeared as they had just been cut. Since the pool had been open for at least five hundred years, how can this absence of wear be explained? It may well have been that, when the project had been completed and water had been struck at the bottom, it was found that the flow was too feeble to serve the needs of a large city. While the pool and stairwell remained open as a source for whatever water could be had from the water room, the stepped tunnel was constructed and was found to be a more adequate means for providing water. The relatively modest tunnel proved to be more useful than the grandiose pool.

If the great pool was constructed primarily as a stairwell, as it seems to have been, why was a circular stairway 37 feet in diameter felt to be necessary? A much smaller cutting would have sufficed for a stairway leading to the artesian water below. Actually a more economical method, that of tunneling, was employed for penetrating below the floor of the pool. There are two possible explanations for this seeming waste of effort.

It is possible that the constructors of the cylindrical pool struck water at the fortieth step, or the level of the bottom of the pool. Later, the water table of the hill dropped and a less ambitious, or more practically minded generation extended the stairs by means of the tunnel without remov-

17. "Gibeon, the vine[yard of A]mariah" scratched on two fragments of the same handle.

18. Photograph and drawing of a handle marked with the names of Gibeon, Domla, and Shebuel.

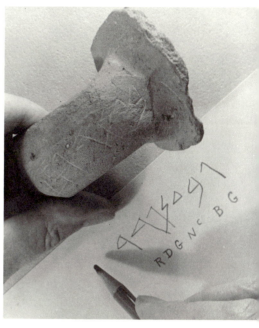

19. The labels were written from right to left in the archaic Hebrew script of the seventh century.

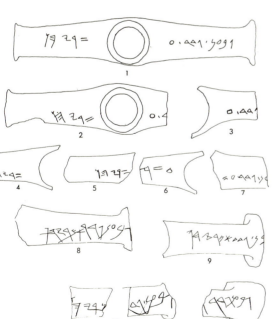

20. Differences in handwriting can be seen from the drawings. The scribe of Azariah (1-7) wrote with a neat, minuscule hand, starting on the lower part of one handle and continuing across the mouth of the jar to the other.

The Amariah scribe (9-14) used only one handle for his label and gave longer descenders to his letters. Hananiah (15) always wrote half of the label on one handle, then turned the jar 180 degrees, and finished on the other handle. His hand is firm and large.

21. Clay stoppers found in the debris with the broken jars.

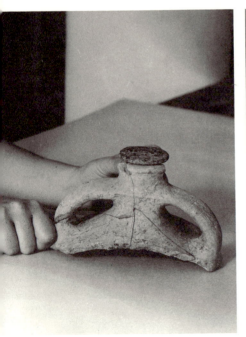

22. A stopper fitted into the mouth of a jar with inscribed handles.

23. A funnel fitted into the mouth of a jar. Both funnel and jar appear to have come from the same potter's shop.

24. Foundation courses of the city wall, which is about 25 feet wide at this point, and the opening to the tunnel with 93 steps leading to the spring.

25. The long corridor of the stepped tunnel is roofed by large stones set in a corbéled construction and covered over with dirt as a camouflage. The arched cutting in the rock at top of the photograph is the boring which goes directly under the city wall.

26. The main corridor of the stepped tunnel. At the lower end of this segment the tunnel turns sharply to the left.

28. The opening of the cistern room to the plain. At the left wall (A) and in the floor (B) are the deep notches into which stones were fitted in time of attack to provide a barricade. The pipe and the masonry wall (C) are recent adaptations.

27. Well-worn steps of the main corridor of the tunnel. The sides of the walls have been polished by the hands of water carriers who braced themselves in their descent to the spring.

29. The cistern room in which water collected from the spring. The water generally came to the top of these narrow steps which led to the tunnel. The small hole in the floor is a settling basin.

30. The rock-cut feeder tunnel extends 112 feet into the hill. A workman cleans the fissures in the rock from which the water flows into the channel.

31. The large pool was cleared of approximately 3,000 tons of rubble by passing it in baskets up a line of workmen deployed on the stairway.

32. An attempt at the removal of debris by means of an A-frame with rope and pulley failed after a short try; the workmen at el-Jib were not efficient in the use of mechanized methods.

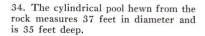

34. The cylindrical pool hewn from the rock measures 37 feet in diameter and is 35 feet deep.

33. Stones too heavy to be placed in baskets and passed along the line were carried up the steps by workmen.

35. At the bottom of the pool the circular stairway continues by means of a tunnel (left) downward for another 45 feet. Under the ladder are two vertical shafts which provide light for the lower reaches of the tunnel.

36. When the break-through was made into the water room workmen found two almost complete jars which had been left by the last users of the system. Light in the foreground is from the shaft under the highest part of the ladder in Fig. 35.

37. Wall of a pool of the Roman period lying in the plain to the northeast of the village spring. Two rows of pottery jars are imbedded in the wall.

38. A smaller reservoir built and plastered in the Roman period to hold the overflow from the spring of the village.

39. A plastered pool or bath of the Roman period, with steps leading down to the basin at the bottom.

40. A hoard of coins, dated to the time of Alexander Jannaeus, 103-76 B.C., found on the floor of a room which adjoined the Roman bath.

ing the central core of the rock, as their predecessors had done.

There is another possible explanation. The construction was begun with a plan to carry the cylindrical cutting all the way down to the water level. When the project was about half finished there was a political or economic disturbance at Gibeon which necessitated the completion of the work on a much less spectacular scale than had been planned originally. It could have been that labor became more costly or that available manpower was reduced through plague, war, or famine when the quarrying had reached the fortieth step. Or the alteration in the original plan may have been due to the rise of a new king or a change in dynasty. Some social change seems the most likely explanation for the alteration in the method of construction which occurred when the project was but half finished.

The season in which the pool was cleared had begun with only a skeleton of a staff. Its modest objective had been that of tidying up what had been begun the previous year. It turned out to be by far the most exciting of our four campaigns. New staff members had to be added to cope with the unexpected wealth of inscriptional material that was imbedded in the fill of the pool. There were long sessions lasting well into the night, when we sat reading the inscriptions that had come to light during the day. And the suspense of following a spiral stairway down step by step with no idea of what might be at the end was exciting for both staff and laborers.

There were some rich by-products of the process of recovering the monumental pool at Gibeon. The jar handles with the names of Gibeon and certain inhabitants of the seventh century b.c. have already been mentioned. Since the pool had served as the city's dump heap for several centuries it was a valuable source for the kind of evidence for a reconstruction of the past which the more sophisticated chroniclers take for granted and fail to record. We shall mention below in Chapter v much of this evidence from the pool: cooking utensils, plates, jars, juglets, pins for clothing, cosmetic instruments used by women to paint their faces, tools, implements of war, importations from Assyria and from Syria, and examples of folk art. This wealth of evidence, which was discarded when broken or lost, is invaluable to the historian because of its unconscious witness to the way in which people lived.

When we began work at el-Jib in 1956 there was not a single ancient wall or building visible on the hill. With the exception of bits of broken pottery every evidence of ancient occupation had been covered over. However, in the open plain to the northeast of the spring of the village an ancient structure was standing. It is a rectangular reservoir or tank, measuring 37 by 60 feet, which had undoubtedly been used to catch and to contain the overflow from the spring.

Robinson noted this structure and surmised that it may well have been the celebrated "pool of Gibeon." Since this had been the only possible candidate for identification with the famous landmark mentioned in II Samuel 2:13 until our discovery of the pool on the hill itself, it was only natural that Robinson's suggested identification should have been followed. The most competent of modern geographers of biblical Palestine, F. M. Abel, believed that the setting of the gruesome contest between the partisans of Saul and those of David took place at the "great waters of Gibeon," of which the present ruined reservoir in the plain is but a "pale souvenir."

One of the high priorities on the list of objectives for our first season of work was the exploration and excavation of this reservoir. It was completely filled in with dirt, except for the upper part of the rim, which served as a fence for the orchard of fig, almond, and plum trees which were rooted in the rich sediment of the pool. This small plot of only one-twentieth of an acre was owned by four different individuals in el-Jib. The boundaries were not marked, but kept in the minds of the respective owners of the trees. We rented a small area at the eastern corner of the reservoir and made a sounding along the wall which ran along the northeast side, a location at which we had to sacrifice only a vine and two trees.

The depth of the reservoir was found to be from 6 to 8 feet. The floor consisted of four coats of lime plaster laid directly on bedrock. The layers of plaster, each of a slightly different color, suggest that the pool may have been repaired on three different occasions. The lowest layer of plaster was of a type widely used in Roman times. The walls of the reservoir were of roughly hewn stones set in mortar and coated with layers of hard plaster.

A unique but puzzling feature of this reservoir was discovered in the sounding beside the wall. When we had chipped the outer layer of plaster from the wall there appeared holes, spaced at intervals of approximately 2 feet and 5 inches, around the upper part of the reservoir (Fig. 37). Below this line of holes was a second line, in which the holes apparently were also evenly spaced around the four walls. When we discovered the upper row of openings in the masonry of the walls, we thought immediately that they were drains to take care of the overflow. But when we probed them more deeply it was apparent that the openings came to a dead end. They had been formed, in fact, by imbedding pottery storage jars, approximately 8 inches high, in the masonry of the wall when it was constructed. Since these vessels were uniform in size and shape, it seems likely that they had been made expressly for the purpose to which they had been put. When fragments of the rim of one jar were chiseled out of the masonry and studied more carefully, we concluded that the jar fitted best into the period from the first century B.C. to the end of the first century A.D.

The function of these openings remains a puzzle. No parallel for this feature of the construction has yet been found; and we have been unable to think of any utilitarian purpose which they could possibly have served. We have continued to refer to these perplexing holes in the sides of the reservoir as "soap dishes," a facetious suggestion of a distinguished visiting archaeologist, who was similarly baffled by them.

Even though the function of the jars imbedded in the walls of the reservoir cannot as yet be explained, they do serve to date rather precisely the construction of the walls to the Roman period of occupation. There was not the slightest indication within the debris around the reservoir that it belonged to Israelite times. This negative evidence, when combined with the positive indication of a Roman date for the walls, is sufficient to render invalid the century-old identification of this reservoir with the "pool of Gibeon" belonging to the time of David.

There is no mention of Gibeon in the written sources preserved from the last two centuries B.C. through the first century A.D., with the exception of the statement in Josephus that Cestius camped there in A.D. 66. In view of this failure of the writings of these centuries to mention Gibeon it was a surprise to discover that there had been an extensive settlement at el-Jib in the first century B.C.

The city of the Roman period was without a wall. On the west side of the hill we found a complex of houses that could be dated by a hoard of coins of the time of Alexander Jannaeus, whose dates are 103-76 B.C. (Fig. 40). Someone had buried twenty-three coins in the corner of a room for safe keeping; there they had remained until a workman obtained *bakshish* for discovering them in 1956.

An interesting feature of the buildings in this period is a plastered pool, or bath, with steps leading down from the top to the bottom, which is 7 feet below the surface (Fig. 39). The steps, sides, and bottom are covered with layers of ashlike plaster similar to that found in the pools discovered in Herodian Jericho in 1951 and at Qumran, the settlement of Essenes who produced the Dead Sea scrolls. Unlike the pools at Jericho and Qumran this pool could not have been filled with fresh spring water, since it is located on the mound high above the level of the springs that flow from its base.

The Roman occupation of the extensive mound was not limited to the west side. In each of the areas that we have excavated on the east side there is considerable evidence for occupation in this period. The remains included houses, plastered conduits, a small stepped pool, which was also plastered, and an Iron Age wine cellar, which had been plastered and used to contain a liquid, in all probability olive oil. The finest collection of Roman jars which we have thus far found was lying on the floor of this storage tank. Undoubtedly, Gibeon was also a great city in Roman times, even though practically no mention of it survives in written history.

The last bit of evidence in the long history of the water system at Gibeon consists of a small reservoir which adjoins the southeast corner of the larger Roman reservoir in the plain (Fig. 38). It is roughly oval in shape, measuring 11 by 17 feet, built of two rows of hewn stones, and plastered with good mortar. It, like its larger neighbor, served to collect the excess water that flowed from the spring of the village. It was free of debris and thus seems to have been used in modern times. Although there are no sure clues by which it can be dated, it seems likely that it was built and used after the larger pool beside it had fallen into disuse.

The efforts which the Gibeonites made to protect and to conserve their natural water resources over many centuries renders most fitting the characterization of "drawers of water," the phrase by which they were perhaps best and longest remembered.

CHAPTER IV

THE MAKERS OF WINE

These wineskins were new when we filled them,
and behold, they are burst.—JOSH. 9:13

T H E Bible has not a word to say about what happened in
Gibeon throughout a span of almost four centuries. The city
had been prominent in the stories about Joshua's conquests
and it had reappeared in the accounts of the internecine
struggles that had taken place during the reign of David.
But for the period extending from the middle of the tenth
century, when Solomon left Gibeon to perform his sacrifices
at his newly built temple in Jerusalem, down to the beginning of the sixth century, when the exile began, there is a
total eclipse of light from the Bible upon the fortunes of
this once celebrated city. From a study of the biblical
sources one might conclude that Gibeon had been a desolate
ruin throughout these centuries.

Excavation has served to fill in the gap. One of the
significant findings of four seasons of work at el-Jib has
been that, in this very period for which the Bible tells
nothing about the fortunes of the city, Gibeon flourished
and reached a peak of prosperity never attained before or
after. Furthermore, it has become apparent that at least one
reason for Gibeon's prosperity was the success of some of
its enterprising citizens in the making and the export of fine
wine. Gibeon may be said to have been an ancient "Bor-
deaux" of Palestine.

The picture of the thriving wine industry did not appear

before our eyes suddenly. Bits of evidence emerged piece by piece over the four campaigns as clues in the identification of what appears to be the oldest winery yet discovered. We shall describe the individual discoveries as they were made and then attempt to put them together in the pattern that was in the end inescapable.

When we had completed the first two seasons of digging at el-Jib it seemed plausible to us that the jars with inscribed handles could have been used for exporting wine from Gibeon to neighboring markets. But there remained the question, of where and how the wine had been made. All the evidence that we had at that time came from the great pool, a receptacle into which the Gibeonites had thrown their refuse after it had ceased to be used. During the first season we had probed the area to the east of the pool, from which the debris might have come; but there was nothing which could possibly have suggested the existence of a winery. No wine presses were found cut in the rock; there were no vats for fermentation; nor was there evidence of any provision for storing wine.

Had it not been for a broken funnel found in the refuse along with the inscribed jar handles, the wine jars could have been considered as having been imported from a neighboring city. In fact, before the evidence of the funnel was published, Karl Elliger, a well-known German biblical scholar, wrote that the name Gibeon on the handles found at el-Jib served as proof that the site of ancient Gibeon was to be located elsewhere. A lone funnel was indeed meager evidence to have survived as the sole remnant of the elaborate equipment which would have been required for the operation of a wine industry of sufficient proportion to allow a surplus of the product for export. If there had been a winery at el-Jib, there should be some remains of the physical equipment used and the remains of it should not be far

41. The wheat field of Jamil Mustafa to the north-west of the pool, where the first Industrial Area was discovered in 1959. The mound (upper right) is debris from the great pool; the square stone (middle left) is the curb to the modern cistern.

42. The area shown in Fig. 41 after excavation. The square stone of the well curb can be seen slightly to the left of center.

43. A wine press cut in the rock, with a segment of a stone trough beside it.

44. A large block of stone, with a hole in the circular trough which would allow a liquid to flow into the basin, may have been used as a dye vat.

45. Holes in the smooth floor of the bedrock: the opening to the left (A) is a wine cellar; the two basins at the bottom (B) may have served as olive presses. Two mortars (C) rest in the rock in the center.

46. Wine cellars were generally covered with a thin slab of stone cut expressly for the purpose.

47. A circular cover to a wine cellar was beveled into the shape of a large stopper to fit into the opening.

48. The openings to a group of wine cellars in the second Industrial Area are inspected by Hassan Abdullah, the owner of the field in which they were found.

OVERLEAF: 49. The first Industrial Area, with its 11 cellars and 11 other cuttings in the rock, lies between the great pool and the modern village of el-Jib.

50. Wine press (bottom), fermenting tank (left), and two settling basins (top) formed a part of the installation for producing wine in the second Industrial Area.

51. The two settling basins are separated by a thin wall of rock through which an opening has been cut —a device for decanting the wine.

52. The opening to a wine cellar of the seventh century had been covered over with stone and cemented
to form the roof of a Roman tomb cut from the rock.

53. Storage jar reconstructed from fragments found
in one of the wine cellars of the Iron II period. The
capacity is 9¾ gallons.

54. Painting from the fifteenth-century tomb of
Nakht at Thebes, with representation of the process
of making wine.

removed from the pool into which the broken wine jars had
been thrown.

It was with the hope of finding an actual winery at
Gibeon that we began in the summer of 1959 to explore the
unexcavated areas adjacent to the rim of the pool. A field
which lay to the south was rented from its three owners
and work was begun in fourteen plots, each five meters
square. When these had been dug painstakingly to bedrock, the results were disappointing. There were only the
most commonplace house walls of the Roman period and
scattered traces of pottery that belonged to three earlier
periods, the earliest of which reached back to the first
occupation of the site at the beginning of the Early Bronze
Age, about 3000 B.C. Alas, the builders of the Roman
period had built too well. They had dug their foundation
trenches down to bedrock, completely demolishing the
earlier buildings as they salvaged all usable building stones.
The first two weeks of this campaign proved to be the
dullest and the most unrewarding period of our entire work
at el-Jib. Yet these weeks were not a complete loss. The
effort did serve to exclude the area immediately to the south
of the pool as a site for the winery, just as the work in 1956
had eliminated the area to the east.

In the third week of the 1959 season it was decided to
move the entire working force to a wheat field which lay
to the northwest of the pool (Fig. 41). The grain was
harvested by Jamil Mustafa, the owner of the land, and the
grid lines were marked out with stakes. This area soon
produced some exciting results. Three inscribed jar handles,
two of them bearing the familiar inscription "Gibeon *gdr*,"
and another incised with the name Hananiah Nera, were
discovered. Since these handles were identical in form and
lettering to the wine jar handles from the pool it seemed
possible that we were at last digging at the place from

which the first and larger collection had come. But our hopes were quickly dispelled by the appearance of the bed-rock lying only 5 feet below the surface of the ground. It seemed that we had come to an abrupt end of our discoveries in this area.

As we were cleaning the bedrock for the final routine of photographing, a workman came upon a well-cut, flat stone, which, when lifted, was found to cover what appeared at first sight to be a cistern hewn out of the live rock. The cover had virtually sealed the opening so that the vat was empty except for a very fine sediment that had washed in through the cracks between the stone cover and rim. The opening was round and measured a little over 3 feet in diameter. Below the stone rim the cutting had been enlarged to a diameter of 6 feet 7 inches and then carried down vertically to form a cylindrical tank that was 6 feet 3 inches deep. The capacity of this jug-shaped cutting was approximately 1,300 gallons. The debris that overlaid the stone cover contained pottery that served to date the last use of the vat to not later than the end of the seventh century B.C.

Could this vat have been a container for wine? A careful examination of its sides and floor revealed that there were no traces of plaster; and one would normally expect to find a trace of lining if the vat had been used to contain a liquid. Yet, since the limestone was close-grained and there were no cracks in the walls, there was the possibility that it could have been used as a wine vat without having been plastered. For several days after the discovery there were long debates among staff members and native residents of el-Jib over the question of the porosity of the rock.

It soon became apparent that only an actual test would be decisive. Happily it was generally agreed that water would serve as well as wine for the experiment. We hired a man to transport water from a cistern two miles away—

water from the spring of the village was entirely too precious to waste merely to satisfy the curiosity of the Americans— and to pour it into the vat. For several days the somewhat bewildered workman drove his donkey with tins of water strapped to its back and emptied them into the hole in the rock in a kind of Sisyphean endeavor. The water disappeared rapidly through the pores of the limestone. It was with considerable disappointment that we were forced to accept the verdict: an unplastered vat could never have contained wine.

As we proceeded to clean the bedrock over an area of approximately 270 square yards we found that it was literally honeycombed with subterranean cavities, all of them neatly hewn from the rock with sharp metal picks or chisels (Fig. 42). Ten more vats were found, each of approximately the same size as the first and identical in shape to it. Our hopes for identifying a wine vat were momentarily raised when one of the cuttings was found to be plastered on the inside and equipped with a curb of stones. But when the stones were demolished tesserae from a mosaic and sherds of the Roman period were found between them. Since the other vats of the same shape had seen their latest use in Israelite times, it was obvious that this ancient cutting had been plastered and reused as a cistern in the Roman period of occupation.

Another of the ancient cuttings in the rock was in use in 1959. It had been cemented and fitted with a curb, to which there had been attached an iron door and hasp. That very spring Jamil Mustafa had channeled water from the late rains into it (Fig. 41); even as we dug in his field Jamil drew out every morning some of the water for his animals.

It was indeed a fortunate circumstance for us that one of these ancient vats had been plastered and was partly filled with water. Our recorder in the 1959 season was R. B. Y.

Scott, an amateur meteorologist who kept a record of the temperature and relative humidity at el-Jib. Scott tied his thermometer on a long string and let it down into the water of the cistern which had been standing there for at least three months. On June 18, where the thermometer registered 83.5° Fahrenheit in the shade of a fig tree nearby, the water in the rock-cut cistern was only 65°—and this particular day was somewhat cooler than the average. Although this observation of the difference between the temperature above the ground and below did not solve the problem of the purpose of the vats, it did suggest that these enigmatic cuttings, when covered over with stone slabs, would have provided excellent refrigeration for whatever had been stored in them.

Since there were no walls of the type usually found in residential areas here where vats and basins had been carved out of the rock, it seemed appropriate to designate it as an Industrial Area. One of the basins, measuring 4 feet by 4 feet 8 inches was hewn out to a depth of about 1 foot (Fig. 43). We surmised that this might have served as a press where grapes were crushed by treading with the bare feet. This interpretation was strengthened when we noticed a small depression, cut into the floor of the basin itself, which could have served to catch the last measure of juice from the pressing. Near the basin was a section of a stone trough, which had once been a part of an installation for channeling a liquid.

At another place in the Industrial Area there was a smaller circular cutting, measuring one and one-half feet in diameter and of about the same depth, which was equipped with a mortar on one side (Fig. 45). This was provisionally designated as an olive press, where olives had been crushed with a pestle in the mortar and the oil had been collected in the basin. Another curious receptacle cut in a large block of stone had a trough which circled the mouth of the opening and a hole which connected the circular trough with the basin (Fig. 44). This device resembled vats which have been discovered elsewhere in Palestine and which have been interpreted by their excavators as dye vats for yarn. The question of what work had been done in the Industrial Area was even further complicated by the appearance of two moveable stone mortars sitting on the rock floor; they could have been used for the grinding of grain or for pressing oil from olives.

An attempt was made to get some clue as to what had been stored in the eleven jug-shaped vats from the residue in them. Samples of scrapings from the walls and the floors of the ten vats—the residue in the one currently used would have been of no value—were collected in plastic jars and rushed to the Government Laboratories of the Hashemite Kingdom of Jordan in Amman. The report of the government chemists showed only that the organic content of these samples was the same as that of the soil which constituted the farm land of el-Jib. Obviously the vats now contained nothing but the dirt which had washed into them through the centuries.

At the conclusion of the excavation of this Industrial Area, we were left with some tantalizing bits of evidence which seemed to defy interpretation. The vats could not have been used for the storage of a liquid in bulk, since they showed no evidence for having been plastered when they had fallen into disuse at the end of the seventh century B.C. They could, however, have served to provide refrigeration or temperature control for whatever had been stored in them.

Wine, grain, and oil were undoubtedly stored in quantities by the ancient Gibeonites, and there were features of the remains in the Industrial Area that might be interpreted

as favoring any one of these commodities as the one proc-
essed and stored there. Yet there were also objections to
each. Grapes could have been crushed in the shallow basins,
of which there were several, but if the juice had been poured
into the vats it would have seeped out as quickly as did the
water which we poured into the vat which we first uncovered. Olives might have been crushed in the smaller
presses, where there were mortars for pounding, and the oil
poured into the vats; but again the porous limestone would
not have contained it for a long period. Furthermore, the
eleven large vats would seem to have been more than ample
provision for the relatively small amount of oil that was
likely to have come from the olive trees of a village of the
size of Gibeon.

A distinguished archaeologist who visited the site as the
vats were being opened up ventured the suggestion that they
had been cut as bins for grain. But two observations made
this theory unlikely. First, the vats were damp and grain
would have mildewed quickly; and secondly, the village
threshing floor lies today on the west side of the hill where
it catches and utilizes the prevailing breeze from the sea. It
is extremely unlikely that in ancient times the grain should
have been threshed and stored in the protected area to the
east of the hill where the vats are.

Thus it was with considerable disappointment that we
were forced to conclude, on finishing the excavation of this
area adjoining the pool, that it was impossible to identify
the product that had been made and stored in the Industrial
Area. Certainly there was no conclusive evidence for a
winery there.

When the areas to the south and to the northwest of the
pool had been explored, we turned to another objective of
the 1959 season: the excavation of the summit of the hill
at el-Jib. It is well known that in ancient Palestine the "high

place" of the city was the place of worship. A look at the contour map of el-Jib showed the highest spot on the hill to be an open field which lay about midway between the east and the west walls of the ancient city. Fortunately, this field was unencumbered by trees or growing crops. Plots were laid out by the surveyor and excavations were begun in a spot which should have been highly rewarding for a knowledge of the cultic life of ancient Gibeon. Our hopes for significant discoveries here were raised by the recollection that the "great high place" at Gibeon is actually mentioned in I Kings 3:4, the account of Solomon's sacrifice there. Furthermore, H. Neil Richardson, while walking about in this very field a month before it was opened, had picked up a jar handle stamped with the royal stamp containing the place name Ziph. If such treasures of the seventh century B.C. could be picked up on the surface, certainly excavation should yield a rich harvest. Four plots were begun there with great expectation.

A week of work produced some strange results. Pottery from the Iron Ages and from both the Early and Middle Bronze Ages appeared, but it was unassociated with house walls and floor levels. Sometimes the earliest pottery appeared on top of later fragments; it was as if the debris had been churned up in some violent manner. A student supervisor encountered a puzzling stone structure which he hopefully spoke of as an "Israelite altar." Finally on July 17, at a depth of just 3 feet below the surface, a workman came upon a brass object, which, fortunately before it was taken from the ground, was identified as a three-inch British shell, unexploded. It was removed by Abu Ali, our representative from the Department of Antiquities, with as much care as would have been exercised upon some delicate archaeological artifact and carried off as a present to the local commander of the National Guard. It was later learned that the "detonation squad" carried the shell to a nearby cave and, after building a fire near the door of the cave, pushed the coals inside and retreated to witness the explosion from a safe distance.

This unusual piece of archaeological evidence from the recent past induced R. B. Y. Scott to search out the official records of the war of 1917, which confirmed that el-Jib had been the principal bastion of the Turkish defense. Although the British held Nebi Samwil, on November 21, they were unable to take el-Jib until December 28. Obviously the Turks had dug in at the "high place"—the student supervisor hastily reinterpreted his "Israelite altar" as a Turkish gun emplacement—and the British had succeeded in virtually pulverizing by shell fire from Nebi Samwil the stratification within the area in which we had placed so much hope. It was apparent that an archaeologist must know his historical sources, both early and late. The plots were discontinued and a new area was attacked.

In a Near Eastern country such as Jordan an archaeologist learns quickly to turn a deaf ear to local rumors about ancient wonders that lie underground. Too often these alleged treasures have been found to exist only in hearsay embroidered by folk imagination. Yet what seemed to be only a highly improbable tale supplied the clues for identifying the winery at Gibeon.

After we had worked for two months in 1959 to discover the inconclusive Industrial Area and the fiasco of the ancient "high place," Hassan Abdullah, an elderly laborer, told me a story to which I had listened patiently but with mounting skepticism on two previous campaigns. Some sixty years earlier, Hassan said, someone in the village had found a great pit in a field of which he was currently the owner, and, upon descending into it, had discovered a cave to which there was a sealed door. Asserting that the story was true "by Allah," Hassan urged me to rent his field for excavation.

By chance on the very day of Hassan's third recital of this story, we had a supervisor and ten workmen who had just finished a plot and had nothing to do. Why not, I thought, put an end once and for all to this improbable legend? Hassan and another villager, whose memory obviously reached back sixty years, solemnly pointed to the spot at which the pit had been seen. We rented the land, staked out a plot of the standard dimensions, and began to dig.

To the amazement of everybody, except Hassan Abdullah and his aged friend, we soon struck the opening to a pit, which was seen to be identical to the vats discovered in the first Industrial Area. Hassan had led us to the discovery of the second Industrial Area, which in many ways was identical to the first but contained features of construction and artifacts that served to clear up many of the perplexities that confronted us in the earlier discoveries (Fig. 48). Throughout the remainder of the 1959 season and most of the 1960 campaign we worked to excavate the second Industrial Area, which lies some 200 feet to the south of the pool. This industrial site is 837 sq. yds. in extent, about three times the size of the site of our first discoveries to the northwest of the pool.

Here the familiar jug-shaped cutting in the rock showed up with almost monotonous regularity. A small plot, only 5 meters square, frequently contained as many as three, and sometimes four, openings in the rock floor, which was almost completely undercut with vats. So close together had these cylindrical chambers been constructed that it was often possible to climb from one to another through a hole which the rock cutters had cut into the wall of an adjacent vat.

When the second Industrial Area had been excavated the

tally showed a total of fifty-two vats which had been carved from the bedrock in this area. When these are added to the number found to the northwest of the pool there was the impressive total of sixty-three cuttings of similar shape and design about which it is possible to make some generalizations. Although some of these had been adapted to other purposes in the course of the centuries (Fig. 52) and others were currently being used as cisterns and were thus inaccessible for exact measurements, fifty-three of these vats provided exact data for sections and plans. The generalizations given below are based on this representative sample from the whole.

The vats averaged 7 feet 3 inches in depth; one was only 3 feet deep—probably unfinished—while the deepest extended downward for 10 feet 6 inches. It is not improbable that the depth was determined by the height of a man. It is possible for a man of average height, while standing on the floor and without using a ladder, to lift a heavy jar from the average sized vat to a position from which it can be taken by another who stands above the opening on the outside. The average diameter of the cylindrical part of the vats is 6 feet 7 inches, ranging from 3 feet 3 inches for the smallest to 11 feet 5 inches for the largest. The diameter of the chamber was probably determined by the extent to which the rock around the mouth could be undercut without weakening the rock which served as a roof.

The openings were made large enough to admit a man, but were kept purposely small so that they might be covered easily by a flat slab of stone. The average diameter of those openings that are preserved in their original size is 2 feet 2 inches. The range is from 1 foot 4 inches for the smallest, to 4 feet 9 inches, the diameter of the largest. In a number of instances a flat stone, obviously quarried for the purpose, was found in place over the opening (Fig. 46). The seal between the stone slab and the mouth of the opening was usually tight enough to prevent much dirt and dust from filtering into the vat. One circular cap was carefully beveled to the shape of a large stopper so as to fit into the opening (Fig. 47). On the edge of this round stone was a slot that had obviously served to receive a lever for prying the stone cover from the opening of the vat. Covers were generally thin and light enough to be moved easily by one man.

At least seven indentations which could have served as lamp niches were observed in walls of the chambers and a number of clay lamps of a type commonly used in the seventh century were found on the floors. Other equipment found in the debris included funnels, bowls, ring stands, and even cooking pots of the Iron II Age. This assortment of utensils of daily use would seem to indicate that these vats may have served as work rooms.

Frequently, as has already been mentioned, there was an opening from one vat into another. Most of the openings between vats seemed to have been accidental breaks, where a stone cutter had hewn too close to the wall of the adjoining vat, but some had been cut deliberately for a purpose that we cannot as yet explain. The best example of an intentional connection between two vats is the tunnel, 2 feet high, which leads from the one to the other. A man could crawl through this corridor, but not with any ease.

One curious feature is the dividing wall which separated an extremely large vat into two parts. There was an opening above to each of these parts of the vat. Since the line of the wall within the vat followed the line of the wall above ground, it is reasonable to suppose that it represented the property line of two owners, and that boundaries to plots of land were considered to extend down vertically. Apparently one could not undermine another's property.

Perhaps the most remarkable feature of these sixty-three

vats is their uniformity of shape. The sections of them appear as so many jugs. They are, without exception, circular in plan; and the chamber of the vat is always of a much greater diameter than the opening at the top. Once the stone cutters got the hole of the opening to a safe distance from the top, they made the roof as near horizontal as they could; the sides were then cut down vertically.

The debris from each of the vats was carefully recorded. Some produced enormous amounts of broken pottery: no less than thirty-four baskets of sherds came from one vat. Of special interest was the pottery from vats that had been covered with a cap stone since their last use at the end of the Iron II period, about 2,500 years ago. In one of these there appeared hundreds of fragments of storage jars, all of them obviously from the same type of vessel; but unfortunately the jars had been so completely smashed to bits that it was impossible, even after days of jig-saw puzzle work, to restore a single one to its original shape. Luckily, however, a complete jar, only slightly broken, appeared on the floor of another chamber which had been tightly sealed for two millennia and a half (Fig. 53).

The jar was repaired sufficiently to contain the sawdust which we poured into it in order to measure its capacity. This storage jar, a little over 2 feet high, was found to have a capacity of approximately 9¾ American gallons. The great quantities of fragments of broken storage jars found in a number of the vats were seen to belong to this standard type of jar. Thus, it became clear that the vats had been used for the storage of some liquid, not in bulk, but in these large containers which had been lowered through the narrow mouth of the vat and stacked in rows around the cylindrical chamber (Text Fig. 7). The height of the vat would easily accommodate two layers of the stacked jars (Text Fig. 8). On the basis of a conservative estimate the

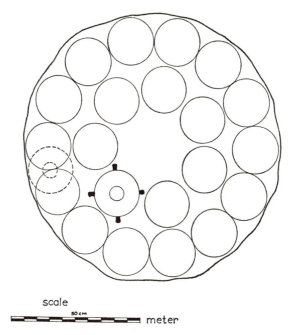

scale

50 cm

meter

7. Plan of the floor of a wine cellar of average size with
storage jars in place. The dotted circles represent
a second layer of jars.

sixty-three vats could have accommodated enough jars to
store in excess of 25,000 gallons of liquid.

But what had the storage jars contained? Two valuable
clues came not from el-Jib but from a Trappist Monastery
at Latrun, some thirteen miles to the west. The principal
industry of the Trappists is the making of wine and brandy.
On a Wednesday afternoon in the 1959 season, a day that
was given over each week to recording and interpreting the
discoveries, the entire staff visited the winery at Latrun for
the purpose of discovering how wine was currently produced
in Jordan.

When we asked how wine was stored at Latrun, we were

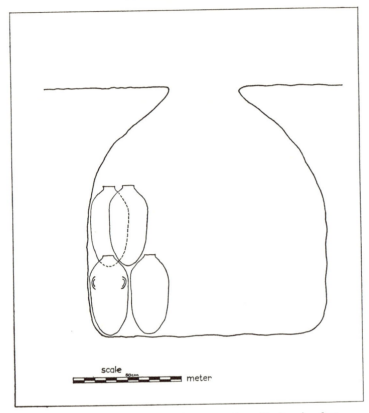

scale

meter

8. Section of a wine cellar of average size with jars in place.
The 63 cellars could have held 25,000 gallons
of wine stored in this fashion.

shown the underground cellars, where the temperature
registered 65 degrees, exactly the figure which we got for
the temperature of the underground vats at el-Jib. If this
temperature is the optimum for the storage of wine today,
could it not have been equally favorable in ancient Gibeon?
It was after this trip to Latrun that we began to call our
juglike vats "cellars."

If wine had once been stored in the cellars within large

jars, for which we now had considerable evidence, how were these jars sealed? The chief wine maker at Latrun made a suggestion: perhaps olive oil had been floated over the top of the wine to keep out the air and bacteria which would have turned the wine into vinegar. We decided to make an experiment. Three bottles of Latrun wine were purchased. Two were opened, and into the neck of one of them we poured a small quantity of olive oil. All three bottles were placed in a cool place.

At the end of a month the staff assembled for a wine tasting party. The verdict was unanimous on two counts: first, the wine in the opened bottle without olive oil had turned completely sour; secondly, it was impossible, except for the taste of the olive oil which could not be entirely poured off, to distinguish between the quality of the wine coming from the freshly opened bottle and that which had been sealed for a month with a layer of olive oil. We left the party convinced that at least it would have been possible to preserve a jar of wine with olive oil poured into the neck to provide an air-tight seal.

These two observations picked up at Latrun and the result of our experiment strengthened the case for a winery at Gibeon. There were several wine presses, an abundance of wine cellars for providing storage space at a constant temperature for the product, and large jars that had been stored in the cellars. Furthermore, these jars could have been made airtight by the relatively simple method of floating olive oil, a commodity easily available in the period from which our evidence came, on top of the wine.

Another link in the chain of evidence for the wine industry appeared in the season of 1960. Over a year after the first wine cellars had appeared at el-Jib, we encountered the first suggestion for the actual process employed in handling the juice from the time when the grapes were pressed until it was placed in jars. In one plot, 5 meters square, there appeared an illuminating complex of rock cuttings (Fig. 50). In the northwest corner of the area there was a circular wine press, approximately 3 feet in diameter and 1 foot 10 inches deep. The walls of this shallow basin were slightly undercut below the rim, possibly for the purpose of keeping the juice from splashing out during the treading. About 4 feet to the east of this pressing basin lay a wine cellar of the standard size and shape. Yet, unlike any discovered before, it was plastered, obviously for the purpose of holding a liquid. Between the wine press and the vat there was a shallow basin, which drained into the vat.

The process suggested by these remains can be provisionally reconstructed as follows. When the grapes had been pressed by the feet of the treaders in the basin, the skins, stems, and seeds mixed with the juice were dipped into the intermediate basin, where as much solid matter as possible was separated from the juice. Afterwards it was allowed to run into the plastered tank where the initial fermentation took place. After the grape juice had been converted into wine it was dipped out of the vat and channeled through a trough, cut into the face of the rock, into a filtering basin, where a further refinement of the liquid took place. The filtering system consisted of two cylindrical tanks, about 2 feet in diameter and 2 feet deep. Between the two there is an opening, which may have been a device for decanting the wine (Fig. 51).

The cluster of wine cellars to the south and to the east of this settling device suggests that the wine may have been dipped from the second of the basins and funneled into storage jars, which were then lowered into the cellars and stored for aging and later use. Although wine cellars are cut in the rock on three sides of this installation, the area for 32 feet to the north was found to have no cutting of any kind. It is possible that the grapes were brought in from the north and stored in this open space in front of the press until they were crushed.

Only a little is known from literary and pictorial sources of preclassical times about the process of making wine in the ancient Near East. From the Bible there are a few hints. Wine presses were hewn out of the rock (Isa. 5:2). Grapes were pressed by foot and the garments of the treaders were often dyed red from the juice as it splashed upon them (Isa. 63:3). The crushing season was a time of joy and singing, and the treading was usually done with two or more people in the wine press (Jer. 48:33). In a list of government officials during the reign of David there is an entry which mentions the royal wine cellars: "and over the produce of the vineyards for the wine cellars was Zabdi the Shiphmite" (I Chron. 27:27). From these and other references it seems that the making of wine was an important industry in Israelite times.

Two graphic representations from Egypt have recorded the process of wine making. One is a painting from the fifteenth-century tomb of Nakht at Thebes (Fig. 54), which shows in a panel only a foot high three steps in the process. To the right, two men pick bunches of grapes from an arbor; to the left, four treaders crush the grapes as they hold on to cords attached to a roof over the basin, presumably to keep from slipping on the smooth, wet floor of the press. In the center a workman attends the collection of the juice as it flows from the press; above him are four tall jars with pointed bottoms, in which the juice is being stored for fermentation. Each of these large jars is fitted with plugs or stoppers. In addition to this painting there is a stone relief from the tomb of Mereru-ka at Sakkarah which depicts two musicians beating time to set the pace for those who tread out the grapes.

From the various pieces of evidence—the inscribed jar handles, the funnels and stoppers, the wine presses, storage jars, the fermenting tank, settling basins, and wine cellars —it is possible to describe in considerable detail the way in which wine was produced in Gibeon. The fresh grapes were crushed by foot in the wine presses; when the juice was separated from the skins, seeds, pulp, and stems, it was allowed to ferment by a natural process of fermentation. After it had been decanted it was placed in large storage jars and sealed with a few centimeters of olive oil for storage in the underground wine cellars where the temperature remained at a constant 65 degrees. Wine for export was transferred into smaller jars with labeled handles for transport to foreign markets. These jars were capped with clay stoppers, which were held in place by a cord attached to the two handles.

In view of the magnitude of the installations at Gibeon for the making and storing of wine it is likely that the harvest season took on the aspect of a public festival. The wide open spaces which have been found to surround the presses and the cellars would have provided room for a large number of participants in this autumnal festival of song and dance. It would be strange indeed if the wine-making season should have been other than the festal occasion described in the Bible and depicted on the Egyptian bas-reliefs.

Two clues, known but not recognized before the discovery of the winery at el-Jib, served to strengthen the conclusion to which four seasons of excavation have brought us, namely, that Gibeon was an important center for the production of wine. The very first report on the Gibeonites to appear in the Bible mentions the "wineskins" which they carried on their visit to Joshua at Gilgal. Is this mention of wineskins in connection with the Gibeonites fortuitous or is there preserved in the memory of this ancient story some connection between the Gibeonites and the product for which the city had long been famous? The other clue is the observation that today grape vines grow in great profusion at el-Jib; in fact, in the process of getting at the wine cellars of the seventh century B.C., we had to remove vines with roots that often reached down to the cellars themselves.

Excavation has produced a new chapter in the history of Gibeon. During those almost four centuries for which biblical sources fail us, Gibeon was a flourishing city, surrounded by a massive fortification, and engaged in a profitable commerce with other cities. In the seventh century, and probably long before, wine was produced in great quantities. That which was not consumed locally was placed in a distinctive type of jar, marked with the name of Gibeon and the name of the producer, and sold abroad.

One can only conjecture as to why a city so prominent in the record of the early days of Israel should disappear from the pages of the religious history of the people. Was it that the Gibeonites, so adept at compromise in the days of the conquest and occupied with trade and commerce, as they seem to have been in the seventh century, were neither concerned with nor involved in the religious and national struggles recorded by the biblical writers? Only one prophet is mentioned as having come from Gibeon—and he, Hananiah the son of Azzur, proved to be a false prophet! The story of Gibeon through the crucial years of Israel's history in Canaan seems to have been one of peaceful coexistence and successful industry.

CHAPTER V

EVERYDAY LIFE

Before the silver cord is snapped, or the golden bowl
is broken, or the pitcher is broken at the fountain,
or the wheel broken at the cistern, and dust returns
to the earth as it was. . . .—ECCLES. 12:6-7

T H E written records about Gibeon which have survived
in the Old Testament consist almost exclusively of scenes
depicting significant events in the history of this city: the
making of the treaty with Joshua, the defeat of the Amorite
kings, the contest between Joab and Abner, the assassina-
tion of Amasa, the execution of Saul's sons, and the sacrifices of Solomon. These are remembered incidents in which
national heroes played a part. They were carried along in
oral tradition until they were finally incorporated into the
national epics of Israel.

These vignettes of memorable episodes from the city's
history can be filled in with details of everyday life, which
the ancient writers took for granted, but with which the
modern reader is frequently unfamiliar. Archaeology is
concerned not only with the great moments in a people's
history but with the way in which the common man lived.
It is from the dump heap of broken and discarded artifacts
that the archaeologist is able to piece together a reliable
picture of how the common man safeguarded his life and
property, what his comforts were, what he considered
beautiful, what contact he had with those who lived outside
his city, what he feared and worshiped, and what were his

resources for providing himself and his family with food and shelter. In a search for this type of historical information hundreds of tons of debris have been sifted and the pieces of evidence have been fitted into a mosaic that portrays the mentality, skills, and interest of people who left no other record of the daily routine of their lives. The miscellaneous assortment of artifacts that have survived the decay of centuries introduces us to the people who once made use of them. In this chapter we shall rely chiefly upon those objects that have come from the Iron Age, a long period extending from about 1200 to 600 B.C. and of principal interest for biblical history.

On our first visit to el-Jib in 1955 we could see the uppermost and latest stratum of ancient civilization in a series of modern defensive measures. On the west side of the rocky hill to the north were two gun turrets emplaced in the rock and pointed toward the Jordanian-Israeli armistice line of 1948; and around the rim of the hill to the south, where the farmers of el-Jib have their gardens, were lines of coiled barbed wire held in place by angle-iron posts. Behind this rusty fortification were trenches, frequently cut into the debris left by the modern defenders' ancestors who lived more than 2,000 years ago.

The excavations have made it apparent that the defense of this site has been a perennial problem. The natural hill on which the ancient city stood towers more than 200 feet above the level of the plain. The rocky scarp of the hill afforded a measure of protection against hostile armies and bands of raiders who passed along the routes of the plain, but in the heyday of Gibeon's prosperity, the Iron Age, further defense was needed. The rim of the natural rocky scarp of the hill was cleared to bedrock and upon this firm foundation a rampart was built. The summit of the hill was circled by a wall of solid masonry; the city built on the top of the hill was converted into a fortress with gates to shut against the enemy, and towers to mount watchmen (Fig. 55).

The Iron Age wall has been traced on two sides of the hill for a total distance of approximately 165 yards. The entire circuit of this fortification measured 1,105 yards, to judge from the circumference of the contour on which the excavated portion of the city wall lay. The width of the wall varied from 10 to 13 feet.

It is impossible to know how high the wall stood, since only the foundations remain. Yet these surviving stubs of the city's defense system tell something of the care with which it had been built. Large blocks of cut limestone—not infrequently do they measure two, or even three feet on a side—were laid in regular courses, of which as many as three were found in place on the bedrock. The facing stones on the two sides of the wall are usually larger and better cut than those which make up the core. A wall built of such large blocks of cut stones could have stood to a height of from two to three times its width, i.e. from 23 to 35 feet.

The ways in which city walls in Palestine were finished at the top can be surmised from two ancient pictures. If the wall at Gibeon followed the style of Canaanite walls of the fourteenth to the twelfth centuries as depicted on the Egyptian reliefs of Seti I and Ramses III, crenelations in stone along the outer edge of the top served to protect the defenders of the city as they fought against the enemy (Fig. 56). But if the top conformed to the style pictured in the Assyrian reliefs of the eighth century, it had a frame of wood in which disc-like objects, or shields, were set to provide protection for the defenders of the city.

Two of the sources for the large blocks used in the wall have been discovered. One quarry was the great pool—

note the balustrade of the stairway where there is evidence for the removal of rectangular blocks of stone—which surely produced much of the stone for the fortification at this vital segment. The other source for stone was a soft vein of limestone on the west side of the hill, where the stonemason's cuttings are still to be seen. This quarry supplies some information on how the stones were removed. Deep grooves were cut into the bedrock so as to isolate the block on four sides. The stone block was then pried loose by wooden wedges driven into the grooves and then wet with water to cause the wood to expand. Deep grooves cut with a metal chisel still remain in the quarry on the west side of the hill.

Towers were built into the wall at one strategic turn in its course. Two of these appear in the segment of wall beside the pool and the opening to the tunnel, a vulnerable part of the defensive system. The towers increased the width of the wall at this point to 23 feet. These two towers served as lookout posts, commanding a view of the main road that passed by Gibeon from Jerusalem to the sea.

The city gate has not as yet been located. From the contour map it would seem that the most likely place for it to have been is at the north end of the mound. Unfortunately this area is now covered by the modern cemetery and is not accessible for excavation.

The dating of the city wall has been rendered difficult by the very thoroughness of its builders. They scraped bare the bedrock for secure foundations and thus destroyed whatever evidence there may have been of previous occupation. However, from the date of the debris that now abuts the lowest course of the wall it seems probable that the foundation of the earlier phase of the wall was built at the beginning of the Iron I Age, perhaps in the twelfth century. It continued to be used, with some repairs and an occasional alteration of its course, until the end of the Iron II Age at the beginning of the sixth century. A road built across a portion of the wall's foundation during the Roman period of occupation indicates that at this time public security was such that city walls were unnecessary.

The building of such a massive fortification at the beginning of the Iron Age, like the excavation of the pool and the subsequent cutting of the tunnel to the spring, must have required a strong local government. It is a pity that history has left no record of the strong leader in Gibeon who looked ahead to see the benefits that this wall would provide for future generations and who mustered the resources for this undertaking. The massive defense system is also witness to the dangers of invasion by powerful enemies in the days of its construction. The absence of any evidence for a general burning suggests that the costly provision which the Gibeonites made for their security was a profitable investment.

Houses in ancient Gibeon were built side by side and often back to back with only very narrow passageways between clusters of dwellings. Space was at a premium within the city wall which encircled the top of the hill and houses were packed tightly into this well-fortified bastion.

It is hazardous to guess how many people lived in the city during the Iron II Age. However, if one takes the estimate of W. F. Albright for the corresponding period of occupation at Tell Beit Mirsim and makes allowance for the larger area of Gibeon—the wall at Tell Beit Mirsim enclosed some seven and one-half acres and that at Gibeon, about sixteen—the estimate would be between 4,000 and 6,000 inhabitants.

A house served a rather limited function and was far from being a home in the modern sense. Like the caves in which man lived in Paleolithic times the houses of the Iron

Age provided shelter against storm and rain during the winter months for the family and domestic animals and permanent storerooms for food and simple possessions. When the house plan of a typical present-day dwelling at el-Jib is compared with that of one of the eighth-seventh century there is a striking similarity between the two.

The rooms of the house of an ancient Gibeonite were not cheerful places, since there was no light within them except that which came in through open doors. Women visited with their neighbors at the village spring, as they do today at el-Jib; and men gathered for business and conversation at the city gate or in some other open space within the city. In all seasons except the rainy winter months, people spent much of their time in the fields and orchards sitting under the vine and the fig tree. At the harvest season families often lived in temporary booths in order to keep a watch over their crops.

A comparatively elaborate Iron Age house of the seventh century was discovered in 1959 near the great pool (Figs. 57, 58). It consists of three rooms built around an open courtyard, which was entered from the north. On the right of the court, as one enters the complex of rooms, there is a small room (124), measuring 5 by 10 feet. In one of the well-built doorposts of the room there is a notch for bolting the wooden door, which once swung on a socket of stone imbedded in the floor beside the opposing doorpost (Fig. 60). At the northwest corner of the room there is a depression, two inches lower than the floor, and edged with a row of stones, which probably served as a bin for foodstuff.

The hard-packed dirt floor was strewn with objects that serve to indicate the use which had been made of this room and the approximate date of its last occupation. In one place workmen were able to collect and to count about fifty olive pits. Nearby were two pieces of hard, volcanic stone, each smoothed on one side to a slightly concave surface, which were recognized as the lower parts of hand mills for grinding grain into flour. Other instruments found were a polished flint, which had once been set into a curved bone or piece of wood to form a sickle, a polishing stone, and a sharp bone blade. From the fragments of pottery we were able to identify a pitcher, a burnished eating bowl, a pottery lamp with a high base, and several storage jars. Undoubtedly this small room had been the place where food had been stored, and perhaps prepared, for the last occupants of the house.

The date of the last occupation is fixed by the finding in an adjacent room of a royal stamped jar handle, impressed with the familiar symbol of the beetle and a Hebrew inscription which reads, "for the king. . . ." From the appearance of this same impression on clay at a number of sites in southern Palestine, it is relatively certain that it belongs to the first half of the seventh century B.C. (see below).

Across the courtyard another room (W 121), which corresponds in plan and size to the one to the west, seems to have been a pantry. Its east wall is constructed of two rows of stones instead of the more usual one, but in other respects the room is similar to the one across the courtyard.

At the back of the house a long room (122), measuring 6 by 18 feet, was entered from a doorway on the long side. The west wall of this room is more than twice as thick as any of its other walls, and there was some indication that a stairway once led to the roof or to a second story. On its floor of beaten earth there were articles of everyday life: two hand mills, a piece of bronze, a flint, a pitcher, and a juglet with a bone spatula in the bottom. A loom weight had survived as the only evidence for weaving, which must have been done within the house.

At the east end of the long room there is a small compartment in which there is a well-built storage bin, 4 feet in diameter and 4 feet 5 inches deep, plastered on the sides and the bottom with soft, gray plaster (Fig. 59). No trace remained of what had been stored in the bin, but it had probably been used to contain grain or some other cereal.

Although the roof had completely collapsed, traces of it remained. On the floor there were masses of decayed limestone, or *huwwar*, which had once served as a waterproof coating for the dirt roof of the building. Beneath were bits of carbon lying on the floor. In all probability wooden beams had been set on the tops of the walls to span the shorter axis of the room. Over these rafters there had been placed a layer of branches or matting, which was covered over with a layer of clay or decayed limestone. The roof was then rolled while it was wet to produce a hard surface impervious to rain. A roller in the form of a round column of limestone, with holes at the ends to accommodate the handles, was found lying in the courtyard of the house (Fig. 62). The roof served not only to keep out the rain in the winter, but as a place where people slept in the dry season. This custom of sleeping on the roof is vividly described in the account of Saul's first meeting with Samuel. When they had eaten together, "a bed was spread for Saul upon the roof, and he lay down to sleep. Then at the break of dawn Samuel called to Saul upon the roof, 'Up, that I may send you on your way'" (I Sam. 9:25-26).

Food was stored and prepared within the rooms of the house, but the actual cooking was done in the open courtyard. There was clear evidence of a fire at one spot in the court of the house. Elsewhere within the excavation we found well-built ovens, circular constructions of clay and bits of broken pottery, about three feet in diameter (Fig. 63). These clay ovens were stoked with brushwood and cakes of dried dung and used for the baking of bread as well as for general cooking.

Pottery provides by far the most important evidence for a reconstruction of the past at Gibeon. A conservative estimate of the number of pieces of broken pottery which have come from the four seasons of excavation at el-Jib is in excess of 200,000. Each of these sherds has been washed, dried, looked at carefully by at least four pairs of eyes; and the crucial pieces of evidence have been photographed, drawn to scale, and catalogued. In this vast assortment of potsherds can be seen hundreds of shapes of vessels and types of decoration which reflect both the inventive power of those who made them and the aesthetic appreciation of those who purchased and used them. Pottery is indeed a sensitive index to the successions of cultures represented at el-Jib.

The pottery from the tell, the living areas of ancient Gibeon, was almost invariably broken. Much of it had been discarded anciently after it had become cracked or broken and has been mixed with the rubble on which later houses were built; but some of the pots had been smashed by the fall of a roof at the destruction of a house either by fire or neglect. The unbroken pottery that we found came mostly from tombs cut in the rock, where it had been protected for centuries. On the basis of a whole specimen it is frequently possible to reconstruct a vessel even when only a fragment of the rim and body survive.

The fragility of pottery, which for the ancient user was a hazard, is for the archaeologist a boon. It is precisely because jars did not last long under the strain of everyday use and were replaced by newer styles that the archaeologist can use the anciently useless pieces as a means for establishing a time scale. Distinctive pottery styles have, in the course of seventy years of scientific archaeology in Palestine, been associated with the several periods of cultural history and now serve to identify the principal periods of ancient life. The fragile nature of pottery, along with its wide use even among the poor, accounts for the vast amount of usable evidence that we have recovered for the history and the daily life of Gibeon.

Most of the pottery from Gibeon was thrown upon a wheel. Jeremiah, the prophet, tells of a visit to a potter in Jerusalem: "So I went down to the potter's house, and there he was working at his wheel" (18:3). The word translated "wheel" is literally "the two stones." This dual form of the noun suggests that the device may have consisted of two discs of stone, the lower one served as a socket on which the upper stone turned. The later picture of the wheel propelled by the foot appears in Ecclesiasticus 38:29: "so too is the potter sitting at his work and turning the wheel with his feet."

Clay which had been carefully prepared by passing through settling basins, and mixed with water by treading it with the bare feet, was placed upon the wheel. The centrifugal force generated by the revolving wheel as it turned rapidly modified by the hands of the potter "threw" the clay into the desired form of a bowl, jar, or other container. As the rising walls of the vessel were finished off with a rim or mouth the pot was taken from the wheel and allowed to dry to a leather hardness. If handles were required strips of clay were then attached with a creamlike mixture of the clay and allowed to harden. If the walls or the base were too thick the vessel was again placed on the wheel and the excess clay removed by a sharp instrument held against the surface. Slip was sometimes applied to fill in the open pores of the vessel and the surface burnished with a pebble or shell to produce a smoother appearance.

After further drying to "white" hardness, the vessel was put into a kiln and fired at temperatures which are known to have been as high as 970 degrees centigrade.

Among the various forms lamps are most readily identifiable as to function. Throughout the entire history of Gibeon these were small saucers designed to hold olive oil and a wick, which almost invariably left a deposit of carbon on the edge of the vessel. The evolution of the lamp can be traced from the beginning of the Early Bronze period, about 3000 B.C., down through late Roman times. Most of the stages in this development are represented by examples found at Gibeon (Fig. 61).

The earliest lamps were plain, round saucers. This simple form was modified in the Middle Bronze I period by the pinching of four indentations in the rim of the dish to hold the four wicks of the lamp in place. In the Middle Bronze II period these multiple lamps gave way to a single-wick type, which continued with certain modifications for 2,000 years. In the Late Bronze and Iron I periods the pinched trough for the wick was more pronounced than it had been in the preceding period; and in the Iron II period the simple bowl with the pinched lip was given a heavy, disc base. Although this form is clumsy in appearance the base probably served to make it more stable. Finally in the Roman period the pinched portion of the bowl was closed over completely at the top to produce a spout and the bowl was covered except for a hole which was left for filling the lamp with oil. The styles employed in the manufacture of lamps over a period of 3,000 years provide an extremely valuable index for chronology.

The cooking pot, subjected to daily use and constant changes in temperature, was probably the most frequently broken of all clay vessels. Bases and bodies are invariably coated with a heavy deposit of black carbon left by the fire over which they were placed, so that the function of the vessels is readily identifiable.

In the Middle Bronze period the typical cooking pot was a flat-bottomed, straight-walled vessel of coarse clay, usually ornamented with a raised band below the rim. Sometimes there were holes punched in the wall of a vessel below the rim to allow the escape of steam when the vessel was covered. Its successor in the Late Bronze period had a rounded bottom and a collared rim, a form that persisted in use through the Iron I period. Coarse, gritty paste continued to be employed in the making of cooking pots in order to take care of the expansion caused by the heat of cooking. In the Iron II period cooking pots appear with two handles, frequently marked with a trademark in the form of a cross, and have collars that are profiled or rilled. Some follow the older tradition of a shallow bowl, while others are deep and have a smaller mouth. In the Roman period the form takes the general shape of the Iron II period but the ware is finer and thinner and the body is frequently ribbed.

Large storage jars come from each of the major periods represented at Gibeon. The flat-bottom jars with ledge handles of the Early Bronze period are displaced in the Middle Bronze period by the more graceful round-bottom storage jars. In the Iron II Age grain was stored in hole-mouth jars, while the vessels with smaller mouths were used for water, oil, and wine.

Juglets were used for two purposes. The small bottles with narrow necks were made as containers for ointment or other costly liquid; the long, narrow juglets were used for dipping liquids from storage jars. Frequently a dipper juglet was found at the bottom of a large storage jar to which it had dropped when the stick inserted through the handle of the dipper and over the mouth of the larger jar had decayed.

The custom of making jars with rounded bottoms, suited

to sand and dirt floors, persisted even when the vessels were stored on hard, beaten-earth floors. Pottery ring-stands served to adapt the round-bottom jars to a flat surface (Fig. 64). It is also likely that the pottery ring-stands served to support round-bottom cooking pots in the fire.

Bowls were made at el-Jib in a great variety of forms and sizes. The simple bowl of the Early Bronze period was supplanted in the Middle Bronze period by a more graceful and delicate shape, which was probably in imitation of a metal prototype. These sharply carinated dishes were covered with a cream-colored slip and burnished to a high luster to give the appearance of shining silver. The most characteristic style of the Iron II period is a shallow bowl with four handles, burnished with a spiral line which runs from the bottom of the inside of the bowl up to and over the rim.

The use of decoration on pottery at Gibeon was almost entirely confined to the Late Bronze Age, when circles, diagonals, and panels of plumb-red paint were employed. Paint continued to be used for a while in the Iron I period, but painted designs were virtually unknown in the later periods.

Although metal was used in every period of Gibeon's history, the remaining evidence for it is relatively scant when compared to the great quantities of pottery found. Gold and silver were used only for jewelry. Iron appears first in the Israelite period, when the Israelites learned from the Philistines—"but every one of the Israelites went down to the Philistines to sharpen his plowshare" (I Sam. 13:20) —how to smelt and fashion this metal, which is harder and less expensive than bronze. Bronze, however, was the most frequently used material for tools and weapons. The best specimens of metal objects have come from tombs, where

55. Outside face of the city wall built of blocks of limestone probably quarried from the great pool, which lies just behind this segment.

56. A bas-relief of Ramses III at Medinet Habu pictures a Palestinian city wall with crenelations and towers for the defenders of the city.

57. A seventh-century house with three rooms arranged around an open court, as viewed from the entry to the court.

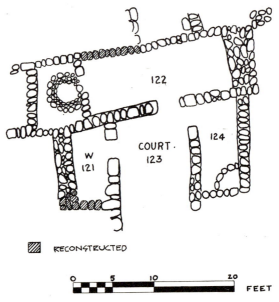

RECONSTRUCTED

0   5   10   20

FEET

58. Plan of the house shown above.

59. Opening off Room 122, a storage room for grain, with a bin that was coated with soft, gray plaster.

60. Rooms were entered by doorways with well-finished doorposts. In one of these there is a notch for bolting the wooden door, which swung on a socket of stone imbedded in the floor by the opposing doorpost.

1

2

3

61. The changing styles in lamps over seven periods of Gibeon's history: 1, Middle Bronze I; 2, Middle Bronze II; 3, Late Bronze; 4, Iron I; 5, Iron II; 6, Roman; 7, Byzantine.

62. A limestone roller for rolling the clay of the roof of the house.

63. A round oven made of clay an broken pottery, used in the Iron I period for baking.

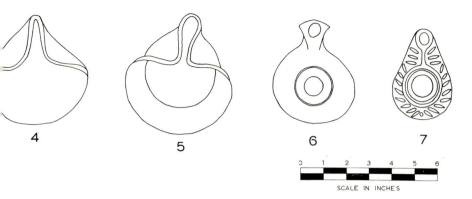

4   5   6   7

SCALE IN INCHES

64. A storage jar with a rounded bottom could be accommodated to the flat surface of a hard floor by means of a pottery ring-stand.

65. A graceful jug (below) of the Late Bronze Age, painted with lines of red and brown paint. This vessel was imported from Cyprus.

66. Small jar (right) decorated with painted triangles and panels inclosing wavy lines, from a Late Bronze Age tomb.

67. Body and base of a decorated mug (left) of the Late Bronze Age.

68. Water flask or canteen (above), of the Late Bronze Age, decorated with circles.

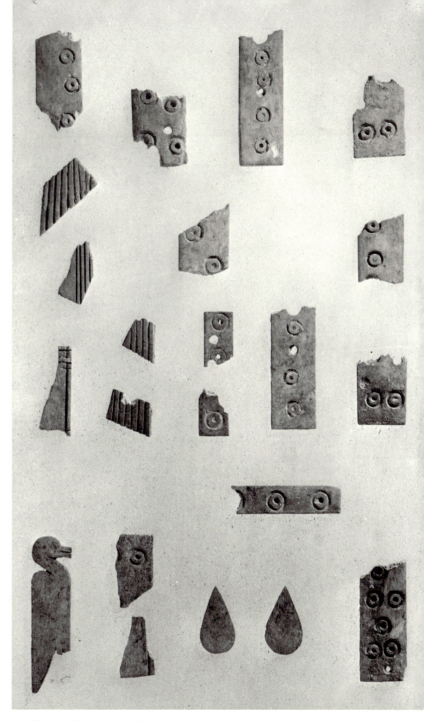

69. Pieces of bone inlay which once decorated cosmetic boxes.

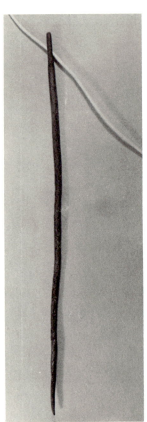

70. A bronze dagger blade and a limestone pommel with hole for attaching it to handle (reconstructed).

71. A bronze needle, six inches long, with a well-formed eye.

72. Bronze spear or javelin point with curled tang for attaching to wooden shaft.

73. Bronze toggle pins used to fasten the edges of a garment.

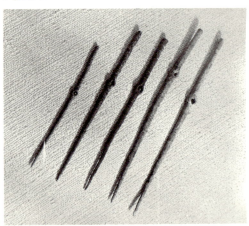

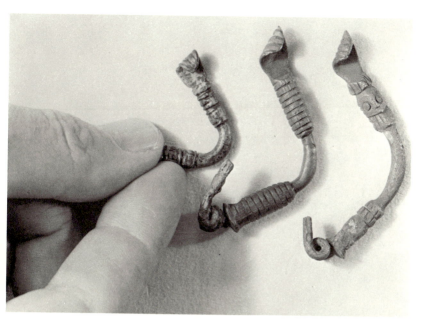

74. Fibulae were the precursors of the safety pin. The sharp pin (now broken away) was clasped by the hand on which the fingers are indicated.

75. Heavy bronze anklets were widely used as articles of personal adornment.

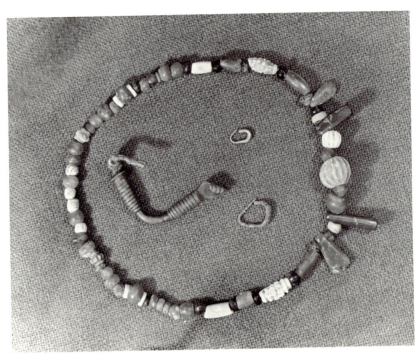

76. A string of beads, a fibula, and two earrings, one of bronze and the other of gold.

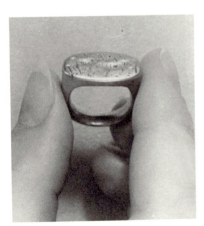

77. A ring of 18-carat gold, weighing 17.2 grams, found in a crack of the city wall.

78. The bezel of the gold ring has two animals carved in a style which suggests Persian origin or influence.

79. A silver ring inscribed with the name of its owner in Aramaic script.

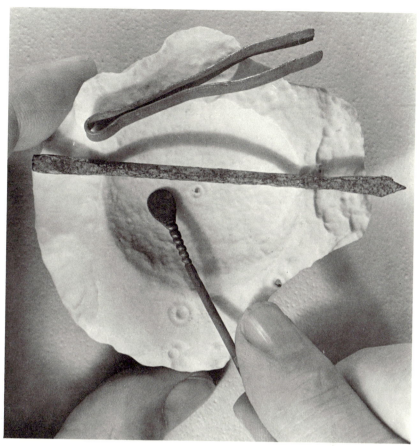

80. A cosmetic palette with two spatulas and tweezers.

81. (Left) Impression of the royal seal with a winged beetle on the handle of a storage jar. Above there appears "for the king," and below there is the place name Memshath.

82. (Above) Impression of the royal seal with a winged sun-disc and the inscription, "for the king, Ziph."

83. A stamp seal of black basalt pierced for suspension, and an impression in plasticene showing three stags.

84. Stone weight of 4 shekels, enlarged to twice size.

85. An impression of a crystal cylinder seal. A worshiper and a stag stand on opposite sides of a sacred tree.

86. Impression in plasticene of a crystal stamp seal bearing the name of its owner.

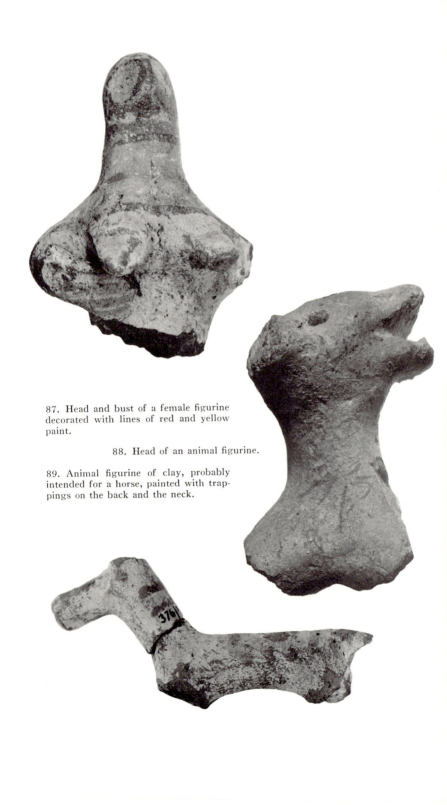

87. Head and bust of a female figurine decorated with lines of red and yellow paint.

88. Head of an animal figurine.

89. Animal figurine of clay, probably intended for a horse, painted with trappings on the back and the neck.

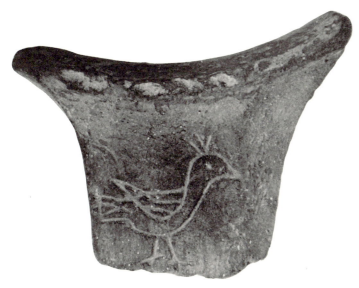

90. A cooking pot handle decorated with an incised bird.

1. Cock incised on the handle of a ooking pot of the Iron II Age.

92. A potsherd incised with a six-pointed star and a bird.

93. A representation of a lion's head once formed a part of a larger object or vessel.

94. Bronze statuette of the Egyptian god Osiris with dowel for attaching to a socket in a stand.

weapons and jewelry had been buried with the dead as part of the funerary equipment. Among the living, metal was carefully guarded, and even refashioned—swords were beaten into plowshares—into new forms. So expensive was metal that the poorer people continued to use the more primitive tools of flint long after the advent of the Bronze and Iron Ages.

The principal use for metal was for tools and weapons. When we opened the Middle Bronze II Age tombs in 1960 we found a number of beautiful bronze dagger blades (Fig. 70). In a Middle Bronze I Age tomb, several centuries older, there was a spear point. The tang of the bronze head was curled, as it had been bent when it was attached to the wooden handle (Fig. 72).

Bronze and iron arrowheads were found on top of the tell, perhaps just where they fell when shot from the enemy's bows. Fighting had taken place also at closer range. An alabaster mace head, bored through to accommodate the slender handle by which it was wielded, serves to illustrate the method of hand-to-hand combat.

The Gibeonite farmer had his tools and some of them have survived. The typical plowshare is a piece of iron, 7 inches long, sharpened to a point at one end and fashioned to receive the wood of the plow handle at the other (Text Fig. 9). From pictures of plowing found in Egypt and

9. Iron plowpoint, sharpened at one end and fashioned to receive the wood of the plow handle at the other.

Mesopotamia, it is known that the plow was in principle not unlike a modern hand plow. It consisted of handles, a beam by which it was drawn by animals, and a small metal point which scratched the surface of the soil like the tooth of a harrow. Soil could not be turned over by such an instrument, but a furrow could be made in which seed could be planted.

A sickle was used to harvest grain. The harvesting instrument was sometimes a curved knife with which the farmer cut the stalks of grain as he grasped them with his hand, but more frequently it was a curved bone or stick into which small flint blades had been set. The flints served to give weight to the sickle and were hard enough to remain sharp even after much use. From the number of sickle blades of flint found it seems that much of the harvesting of grain in Gibeon was done by Stone Age methods.

Bronze needles were used for sewing skin and cloth. One excellent example is six inches long and has a well-formed eye, large enough for a leather thong (Fig. 71). A smaller needle, three inches long, has a sharp point and an eye which was intended for a thread the size of modern darning cotton. It was in as good a condition as when lost centuries ago.

Woven materials were widely used for clothing. Spindle whorls, used in the making of thread, have been found in great numbers throughout the excavation; and clay weights, pierced for a thread, constitute a proof that the vertical loom had been used. In the Bronze Age the toggle pin was used to hold together the ends of sashes and garments (Fig. 73). This device consists of a long needle, the upper part of which is frequently decorated with a pleasing design, with an eye near the middle in which a cord was tied. After the pin was put through the two pieces of cloth so that both ends of the pin were on the outside, the attached cord was wound firmly around the two ends of the pin to form a knot from which it was impossible for the pin to work loose.

In the Iron Age the fibula almost completely displaced the toggle pin as a fastener for garments (Fig. 74). The fibula is a safety pin fashioned into the shape of a bent elbow with a sharp pin across the diagonal. The pointed end of the pin was clasped by a catch in the shape of a human hand. The care with which toggle pins and fibulae were decorated indicates that they served ornamental as well as utilitarian purposes.

The ancient Gibeonites were not exclusively concerned with necessities, such as defense, housing, food, drink, and clothing. They indulged themselves in luxuries and followed the prevailing styles in personal adornment. In Isaiah 3:18-21 there is an inventory of the finery worn by the ladies of Jerusalem: "anklets, the headbands, and the crescents; the pendants, the bracelets, and the scarfs; the headdresses, the armlets, the sashes, the perfume boxes, and the amulets; the signet rings and nose rings." A number of these items are illustrated among the articles of personal adornment found at el-Jib.

Bronze anklets make it certain that Gibeonite women, like their sisters in Jerusalem, walked "tinkling with their feet" (Fig. 75). These heavy anklets—three of them weigh 8 oz.—were obviously attached to the leg by the metal-worker and worn permanently. An exquisite gold earring in the shape of a crescent was found complete with the sharp pin which pierced the earlobe (Fig. 76). Another larger example made of bronze, but of the same design, has remained unbroken; and a third bronze specimen, but with pin missing, has been found. Beads and pendants of carnelian, paste, and other materials were salvaged from the dirt on the floor of the tombs by passing the dirt through a fine wire mesh.

A perfectly preserved signet ring of 18-carat gold, weighing 17.2 grams, was found by a workman from Jericho in 1959 as he cleaned the dirt from a stump of the city wall, which had been destroyed in the sixth century (Figs. 77, 78). The design of two animals engraved on the bezel of the ring is Persian in style. The ring may have been dropped by some official of the Persian satrapy to which Gibeon belonged in post-exilic times; or it could have been the proud possession of someone in Gibeon who had bought it in Persia. A more delicate ring of gold came from a Middle Bronze Age tomb. Unlike the Persian ring, which was cast in a mold, this had been made of fine gold wire and an Egyptian scarab.

In the 1959 season a silver ring appeared which had on the bezel seven Hebrew letters in the Aramean script of the late sixth century. Provisionally they may be read *l mrtsmn*, presumably the name of the owner (Fig. 79). It is clear that the name had not been intended for stamping documents since the inscription is engraved in the normal direction and not in mirror writing, as are stamps. More common than these rings made of precious metal are the many bronze rings, plain and unadorned, which once belonged to the poor.

The women of Gibeon made use of cosmetics and probably plucked unwanted hair with tweezers. Paint for the eyes—Jezebel was long remembered for this display of vanity (II Kings 9:30)—was ground in a small, decorated palette of fine-grained limestone (Fig. 80). One of the two examples of this type of cosmetic bowl is gracefully made and decorated with small, incised circles around the rim. When the *kohl*, or other pigment, had been ground to a fine powder in the palette and mixed with other ingredients, it was applied to the face by means of a small bronze spatula which was sometimes decorated with incised lines around the handle. A pair of bronze tweezers, which could have been used for plucking eyebrows or other hair, were found to be in usable condition. Beauty was purchased by the Gibeonite women at a rather high price of costly bronze equipment.

Gibeon was no isolated, provincial city. Conspicuous evidence for commercial intercourse in the days of the Judaean kingdom is supplied by the royal stamps on jar handles. Eighty of these impressions were salvaged in the first two seasons of excavations. The seals from which the impressions were made bore either the design of a winged beetle (Fig. 81) or that of a winged sun-disc (Fig. 82). Above the design were four Hebrew letters, *lmlk*, "for the king," and below, there generally appeared one of the four ancient place names, Hebron, Socoh, Ziph, or Memshath. The first three of these are well-known towns in Judah, but the fourth is not mentioned in the Bible or in other literature. The handles that bear these impressions once belonged to large, four-handled storage jars which held approximately ten gallons of liquid. Royal stamp impressions like the ones from Gibeon have come from such widely separated sites as Tell Beit Mirsim (33 miles to the south), Lachish, Beth-Shemesh, and Tell en-Nasbeh (3 miles to the north). This wide distribution of remains of large storage jars with similarly stamped handles indicates that there existed a lively trade throughout this area of ancient Judah.

The purpose and use of these royal stamps inscribed with the names of four Judaean cities have been the subjects of debate over several decades. What did these symbols accompanied by the inscription, "for the king," mean?

Two possible answers have been suggested. One is that the stamp was the trademark of royal potteries which were located at each of the four cities mentioned and that the jars were produced for some governmental use, such as the collection of taxes. Another explanation is that the jars were made expressly for a winery under royal patronage in the Hebron area and that the place name on the stamp indicated the region in which the grapes were grown.

A careful examination of the symbols and the writing on a number of royal-stamp jar handles has led Paul W. Lapp to conclude that handles that have come from such widely separated towns as Tell en-Nasbeh, Lachish, Gibeon, and one of the Shephelah tells were all impressed with the same seal.[1] If this observation is correct then the royal-stamp handles provide tangible evidence for trade between these ancient cities in the seventh century B.C., the period to which they are generally ascribed.

One of the seven private-seal impressions on the jar handles that have been found at el-Jib bears the inscription, "Belonging to Tanhum Negeb." When we compared it with a photograph of a similar impression found some thirty years earlier at Beth-Shemesh, we discovered that on both there is evidence of a mistake in the cutting of the border at the lower left-hand side of the seal. The tool had slipped as the engraver was cutting the border of the seal. This defect in the seal makes it possible to identify these two impressions, found 14 miles apart, as having come from the same seal. Obviously the Gibeonites traded with the men of Beth-Shemesh.

A balance with a pan suspended at each end was used for weighing what was bought and sold. A spherical stone weight, flat on one side, was discovered in 1957 (Fig. 84). On its top there is a *g*, to be read as the numeral 4, and an

[1] *Bulletin of the American Schools of Oriental Research*, no. 158, p. 14.

X-sign which is closed at the bottom, the symbol for the shekel. It has been suggested that this sign for the standard Hebrew unit of weight is a pictographic representation of a bag, in which weights or money were carried, tied with a string in the middle. Our stone weight, which is 51.6 grams, is 13 per cent heavier than the average for four other weights marked with the same signs. This variation may mean that there were different standards for the shekel in ancient Israel, or that some seller at Gibeon operated in violation to the command in Deut. 25:13, "You shall not have in your bag two kinds of weights, a large and a small." The earliest coins found at el-Jib are from the third century B.C., from which time they continued to be used down to modern times.

In addition to the numerous impressions of seals on clay, some actual seals have been recovered. The most beautiful is a crystal cylinder, about the diameter of a lead pencil, which is engraved with an Assyrian scene of a worshiper and a stag standing on opposite sides of a sacred tree (Fig. 85). The seal could be suspended about the neck of its owner by a cord which passed through a hole bored through the center of the cylindrical seal. When this engraved cylinder was rolled over the wet clay of a contract tablet it left an impression which was the distinctive mark of one of the contracting parties.

Two stamp seals have been found. One is a piece of crystal, shaped like a pendant, and bored with a hole for suspension about the neck (Fig. 86). The end that was used for making the impression upon wet clay bears a name which we have read provisionally as 'nyhw bn hryhw. The seal is interesting because of a very obvious mistake which appears on it. In order to make the impression come out properly the seal itself had to be cut in mirror writing, i.e., in reverse. It is obvious that the craftsman made a mistake in the cutting of the letter *n*, and cut it as it appears normally and not in reverse as it should have been. Another seal had been made from a piece of coarse basalt (Fig. 83). When the end of the stamp had been cleaned and an impression made on a piece of plasticene the design of three very active stags became apparent. Like the other seals this heavier and cruder one is also bored through for suspension. It belongs to a type of representation common in Palestine in the ninth-eighth centuries.

The Gibeonites of the seventh century were worshipers of Yahweh, god of Israel. Their religious loyalty is best attested by the meanings of personal names that have come from the excavations, either stamped or inscribed on jar handles. Four of these names are in the form of a sentence in which the god Yahweh, in the abbreviated form "-iah," is the subject. Each seems to have been an exclamation which acknowledged the aid of Israel's god. Hananiah means "Yahweh has been gracious"; Amariah, "Yahweh has promised"; Azariah, "Yahweh has helped"; and Hizziliah, a name appearing on a handle stamped with a private seal, obviously means "Yahweh has delivered." The names Nahum, Meshullam, and Elnathan, while of a different formation, all appear in the Bible and are quite proper as names for worshipers of Yahweh, god of Israel.

Some objects found in the same context as that which produced the personal names with Yahwist compounds reveal that the people of Gibeon, while loyal to the god of Israel, may not have been entirely orthodox in their religious practices. No less than fifty-four fragments of fertility figurines were found in the refuse which had been swept into the great pool (Fig. 87). That not a single figurine was found unbroken might be interpreted as evidence for some iconoclastic reform, such as that carried out by Josiah in Jerusalem in 621 B.C., when he cleared the temple of a variety of pagan representations (II Kings 23).

The figurines, which stood to a height of from 3 to 6 inches when whole, represent the female figure with protruding and often exaggerated breasts. Below the bare chest the figure is stylized into a pillar-like support and base. The heads are of two types. In eight examples the head has been made by placing clay in a mold or matrix in which there had been carved delicate facial features and representations of the coiffure above the forehead. In fourteen instances the head was made much more simply. When the potter had formed all except the head he merely pinched the clay at the upper end of the long neck to form a crude, birdlike beak and the suggestions of eyes. The figures were decorated with bands of red and yellow paint applied over a white wash that coated the entire figurine. The neck and head were also frequently painted in gay colors.

Although hundreds of these figurines have been found in Palestinian excavations, no satisfactory explanation of their meaning or function has been determined. Was the figure a doll, a goddess, or a charm? Perhaps the suggestion that they were charms used by women to assure success in childbirth and in the rearing of the child through the crucial months of nursing is the most convincing. Although the meaning of these enigmatic figures cannot be determined, it is certain that they were widely used in the eighth and seventh centuries at Gibeon.

From the same pottery shop that produced the female figures came fragments of seventy animal figurines of clay (Figs. 88, 89). The most common representation is that of a horse with a rider attached to its back. On some examples there are painted representations of either harness or a rug on the back of the animal. One plausible interpretation of these figurines is that they were apotropaic objects; if they were, then the account in II Kings 23:11, of Josiah taking away "the horses that the kings of Judah had dedicated to the sun," may well refer to the removal of figurines like these found at Gibeon.

In addition to representing humans and animals the Gibeonites occasionally incised the handles of their cooking pots with drawings of chickens or birds. Three of these primitive drawings were found on handles of the cooking pots belonging to the Iron II period (Figs. 90, 91). A drawing of a bird was found within a six-pointed star incised on a sherd from a large storage jar (Fig. 92). The appearance of the familiar "star of David" on this fragment, as well as on two other pieces of pottery, is the earliest example for the use of this familiar symbol, apart from its appearance on a monumental structure at Megiddo.

A crude representation of a lion's head, with two warts on the forehead, made of black clay had once formed the part of a larger object (Fig. 93). A bronze statuette of the Egyptian god Osiris appeared in the debris that had filled in the second Industrial Area (Fig. 94); it is obviously an import from Egypt, where these figures were common from 700 to 300 B.C. and even later.

The prevalence of these various representations of human and animal figures made by people who were Yahwists in their religion would seem to exhibit a disregard for the aniconographic command which appears in Exod. 20:4: "You shall not make yourself a graven image, or any likeness of anything that is in heaven above, or that is in the earth beneath, or that is in the water under the earth."

In ancient Gibeon most men were farmers. A few people made a livelihood from working metals, making pottery, or in trade, but the overwhelming majority spent their days toiling by the sweat of their brow to get a living from a soil that was cursed with thorns, thistles, and stones. The farmer had a few animals, such as sheep, goats, cows, donkeys, and domestic fowls, which he kept within the court of his house. Sheep and goats provided wool for clothes and hair for tents, as well as milk and cheese and meat for an occasional feast. Cows and donkeys were used for plowing and for transportation; chickens were eaten. The main concern of the farmer, however, was with providing himself and his family with "wine to gladden the heart of man, oil to make his face shine, and bread to strengthen man's heart" (Ps. 104:15). To the major products of grapes, olives, and grain there should be added honey for sweetening, figs, almonds, vegetables, and spices.

The work of farming was spread over a good part of the year. Nowhere is the unremitting labor required of the farmer better illustrated than in a kind of farmer's almanac, inscribed on a limestone plaque from the tenth century B.C., found at Gezer, only 16 miles from Gibeon. In tabular form the inscription gives a list of what the farmer does month by month:

> His two months are (olive) harvest,
> His two months are planting (grain),
> His two months are late planting;
> His month is hoeing up of flax,
> His month is harvest of barley,
> His month is harvest and *feasting*;
> His two months are vine-tending,
> His month is summer fruit.[2]

The olive harvest comes within September-November, plowing and planting within November-January. Late

[2] *Ancient Near Eastern Texts*, edited by James B. Pritchard, 1955, p. 320.

planting would extend over January-March; the flax harvest would then fall in March-April, the barley harvest in April-May, and the wheat harvest in May-June. The vintage season is July and August, and the month of summer fruit, such as figs, pomegranates, etc., belongs to August-September. Although this enigmatic text is laconic and general, it does show that the farmer managed to keep busy for the entire year with the care of the diversity of crops that grow in the hill country of Palestine.

The women of Gibeon, if they in any way approach the ideal of the good wife described in Proverbs 31, did the spinning, assisted with farming, and even at times supplemented the family income by selling garments and girdles.

CHAPTER VI

THE NECROPOLIS

There the wicked cease from troubling,
and there the weary are at rest.
There the prisoners are at ease together;
they hear not the voice of the taskmaster.
The small and the great are there,
and the slave is free from his master.
—JOB 3:17-19

T O M B S have been discovered at el-Jib from each of six major archaeological periods in the city's history: Early Bronze, Middle Bronze I, Middle Bronze II, Late Bronze, Iron, and Roman. From these burials we have learned that for over a span of more than 3,000 years it was the practice to inter the dead in chambers hewn from the live rock of the hill, and to supply them with food, drink, weapons, clothing, utensils, and jewelry for use in the life of the nether world.

Such well-equipped tombs provide some evidence for men's beliefs about the life after death. The grave was supplied with the things a man had needed in his everyday, secular life; it was believed that he would continue to need the same equipment. Noticeably absent in the tombs were cultic objects, such as figurines and amulets. Apparently life after death was thought of in purely materialistic terms; cultic and magical practices were for the living, not for the dead.

The burial deposit within a tomb is also valuable in illustrating the everyday life of the living within the period in which the burial took place. Most of the objects that may go eventually into display cases of museums to show how people lived in ancient Gibeon will have come from tombs. Fragile objects, such as pottery jars, survive better in burial chambers than they do in the ruins of the living areas of the city. By sifting the dirt from the floor of a tomb it is relatively easy to recover intact such small things as earrings, beads, scarabs, pendants, seals—articles that are difficult to find on the floors of a house or in the dump heap. Thus tombs are the principal source for museum pieces.

The dishes, bowls, and jars of pottery buried with the dead and unbroken in a sealed tomb are useful not only as display pieces but as models for the reconstruction of small fragments of sherds from similar vessels found on the tell. It is not infrequent that the only complete form of a distinctive type of pot, to which many fragments found in a crucial area of the excavation once belonged, comes from a tomb of the period.

More important even than the objects themselves is the relationship established when objects are discovered grouped together within one tomb. Artifacts from a single tomb are homogeneous as to date, barring, of course, the presence of a family heirloom in the collection or the reuse of the same tomb for another burial at a later time. In a single-burial tomb, with its pottery, tools, weapons, jewelry, etc., time stands still, as it were, so that the archaeologist gets an accurate cross section of the culture of that time and place. Obviously no object within a sealed tomb can be later in date than the interment of the body, and the objects found in this association are not likely to have been used for more than a generation or two before they were placed in the tomb. In such a group of related objects the fixing of the date of one object suffices to determine the date of the other artifacts with which it is associated. Tomb groups are most important for establishing chronological relationships.

It must be stressed, however, that the application of this principle of the contemporaneity of tomb deposits is often vitiated by the frequent ancient practice of reusing a tomb. The biblical expression, "and he slept with his fathers," is a literal description of burial custom. In a number of tombs at el-Jib the bones that had remained from one burial were found to have been pushed aside to make room for a new corpse, and this procedure had often been repeated again and again. One small tomb that was opened in 1960 contained the remains of no less than fourteen skeletons.

It has long been known that there were ancient tombs at el-Jib. The Survey of Western Palestine, made in the 1870's, noted thirty-four rock-cut tombs carved into the sides of the hill on which the ancient city stood. Although all of these had been robbed by the time of the Survey, it was apparent from certain characteristic features of construction that they belonged to the Roman period of occupation.

The files of the Department of Antiquities of Palestine, now kept in the Palestine Archaeological Museum in Jerusalem, indicate that from time to time over a period of more than thirty years before our first excavation villagers had been reporting the chance discoveries of ancient tombs. On October 16, 1923, a peasant broke into an Early Bronze Age tomb while digging a trench in which to lay a foundation for his house. The Museum purchased the pottery that came from it. In the fall of 1941 an inspector of the Department visited el-Jib and returned to Jerusalem to report that there were a number of rock-cut tombs on the west side of the tell, some of them with a vestibule leading into a small, square opening and others of the shaft type typical of Middle Bronze Age burials. He also noted that at the southwest side of the tell there were remains of ancient quarrying and that the rock there was honey-combed with tombs. Unfortunately he left no plans, nor did he bother to list the names of the owners of the fields in which the tombs were to be found. Had he been more specific in his report our search for the Bronze Age necropolis might have been made much easier.

A further notation in the records of the Department states that, on November 25, 1941, Shakr Abd el-Hamid found a cave full of pottery and bones. This is apparently the tomb that was cleared by the Department of Antiquities and described by Nelson Glueck as having contained mostly Middle Bronze Age pottery with an admixture of Iron Age II forms.[1]

In the spring of 1949, Mahmud Ahmed Hussein, who lived a short distance to the south of the *ein el-beled*, began to level off the ground behind his house. Before he finished the job he found the opening to a large cave, measuring 27 by 24 feet, with a roof about 6 feet high. He entered and found the cave literally filled with pots. He removed thirty-six of them and promptly reported his discovery to the authorities at the Museum in Jerusalem. About a year later Awni Dajani, then the Inspector of Antiquities for the west bank of the Jordan, began a careful examination of this cave. It proved to be rich in artifacts, although the burials had been completely disturbed. Besides about five hundred pots of various forms, Dajani found rings, earrings, bracelets (of which there were forty-four), anklets, fibulae, toggle pins, needles, arrowheads, scarabs, seals, and dagger handles.[2]

The high proportion of clay lamps, which constituted 45 per cent of the total number of pottery vessels found,

[1] *American Journal of Archaeology*, vol. 47, 1943, p. 127.
[2] *Annual of the Department of Antiquities of Jordan*, vol. 2, pp. 66-74, pls. 9-10; vol. 3, figs. 19-22.

indicated that light in the tomb was thought to be important. Of the 223 examples of lamps recovered not one had the footed base so characteristic of the lamps from the latter part of the Iron II period. Some bowls displayed the marks of burnishing by hand, while others had been burnished on a wheel. These and other indications of date point to an extended period of several centuries within the Iron I and the first part of the Iron II periods when the cave had served as a burying place.

In 1956 we re-entered this tomb and found an area at the back which had not been fully cleaned by the Department of Antiquities in 1950. It was productive of some excellent examples of the type of Iron Age material that had been found during the first excavation. In addition there appeared some specimens of Early Bronze Age ware. Apparently this large cave had been used as a tomb over an even longer period of time than had at first been estimated. By a careful sifting of the debris we were able to recover a number of small objects, such as beads, scarabs, pendants, and the like.

During our first season at el-Jib we organized a "prospecting party" of a half dozen workmen who had lived all their lives in the village and who were entirely familiar with the rocky sides of the tell. If anyone could find the openings to ancient tombs it seemed likely that it would be this group of men, who not only had worked the fields on and around the tell but knew well the village lore about ancient discoveries. Over a period of several weeks this small party and its supervisor reported discoveries of natural caves and rock cuttings, but no trace of tombs. It was perplexing that, with the thousands of burials that must have taken place at Gibeon over many centuries, not one tomb was discovered that season, either by archaeologists or by the villagers.

Four seasons later we were more successful. In 1960, when the Bronze Age necropolis was discovered, it was not found by a member of our scientific staff, but by a native Arab woman. When we were about half way through the season a grandson of Azziyeh Umm Azzat, a venerable lady of the village, brought two easily recognizable Middle Bronze Age jars, which he said belonged to his grandmother. He asked if we were interested in them. Indeed we were! Jars in such perfect condition could only have come from a tomb.

The boy took us to his grandmother, who with considerable pride led the way down the rocky scarp of the west side of the hill to her small plot of vines, tomato plants, and fig trees. There, within her garden, was a tomb, which she had already partly excavated with the hope of finding a ready-cut cistern in the rock where she might store rain water for irrigating her plants during the summer. To the north and to the south of the circular shaft leading to the tomb were other similar openings in the rock. These, she readily admitted, had been excavated some years earlier and had been found to be filled with pottery. She told how she had tried to sell the pots; but when she had been unable to find a buyer she had smashed them all in the corner of her field. There were more tombs in her field, she assured us, and these had never been opened.

We took up the digging where Azziyeh had left off. In the time which remained of the 1960 season we were able to clear eighteen of the tombs that had been cut into the shelf of soft limestone that lies under the shallow soil of Azziyeh's farm.

Only one of the tombs that we cleared that season was tightly sealed. The others were found to be completely silted up with soil that had washed in from above. The soft limestone, which the tomb cutters had found easy to work in the Middle Bronze Age, had given way over the centuries to pressures and decomposition and the tomb chambers had become tightly packed with rocks and soil. By careful digging with small picks, knives, and even brushes we were able to extract many whole vessels and other artifacts which enabled us to date the use of these broken tombs.

Although the tombs vary in size, they are uniform in plan (Fig. 96). Each has a cylindrical shaft, averaging about 4 feet in diameter, cut into the rock to a depth which varies from 1 foot 3 inches to 8 feet 6 inches—the average depth is 6 feet (Fig. 100). At the bottom of the shaft a doorway, averaging 2 feet 7 inches by 2 feet, cut into the side of the shaft, opens into the chamber of the tomb (Fig. 104). The tomb chambers are of various shapes and have an average floor area of 5.94 square yards. In height the tombs vary from 2 feet 9 inches to 4 feet 5 inches, the average being 3 feet 4 inches (Fig. 103). After the body had been placed in the tomb, the doorway to the burial chamber was closed by a large, flat stone and the shaft filled with packed chips of limestone and *huwwar* to make an effective seal.

The best-preserved burial appeared in Tomb 15, where a well-sealed door leading from the shaft into the tomb chamber had kept out the water from the winter rains. It was obvious, even before the door was opened, that the tomb was probably in good condition. Workmen had managed to clear the shaft down to the doorway of the tomb itself by the close of the working day. Understandably both staff and workmen were eager to see what treasures lay behind the sealed door. Yet to open the door late in the day would have provided an opportunity for curious villagers to destroy the arrangement of the remains and perhaps to loot the contents after we had left the site for the day.

To the obvious disappointment of an impatient and excited band of workers the decision was made to postpone the opening until the next morning. The National Guard was asked for sentries and the commanding officer responded by sending two armed soldiers and by assuring us that a sergeant would check on the guards at hourly intervals throughout the night to see that they were awake. Pencil marks were placed on the door and on the sides of the tomb chamber in such a way that any tampering during the night could easily be detected in the morning.

When the time for opening came the following day there was an excited group crowded around the shaft: staff members, workmen, Azziyeh, and even the tired guards, who insisted on remaining to see the treasure that they had guarded throughout the night (Fig. 95). The first look was breath-taking. Here was an undisturbed sample of almost every aspect of the material culture of 3,600 years ago: storage jars, bowls filled with the residue of meat, lamps, perfume juglets, pitchers, dishes, weapons, jewelry, and the long, graceful pins which had once held together the edges of a woven garment. With this rich assortment of articles of daily life, which had been provided for the dead by their survivors, there were the bones and skulls of at least fourteen people for whom this tomb had been a peaceful home for thirty-six centuries. Even though it meant the loss of valuable time, each workman in the area, as well as our valued friend Azziyeh Umm Azzat, was allowed to scramble down the shaft and take a look at a scene which no human being had viewed for centuries.

The process of recording accurately the deposits in a tomb is a slow one. After preliminary photographs were made, our draftsman, Gustav Materna, began the laborious job of measuring the location of every jar, bone, and other object and sketching these in their correct positions on a drawing board (Fig. 97). Nails were driven into the walls of the tomb and a string was stretched to provide a datum line of reference for measuring the location of the objects. Each object was given a number by which it could be identified on the sketch, and then removed for cleaning and cataloguing (Fig. 99). When the upper layer of burials had been completely removed, the process of photographing, measuring, and sketching began all over again, and the second layer of bones and the objects that belonged with them was recorded. Below this phase of use there was a third and final layer. Here for the first time a skeleton was found relatively undisturbed, lying on a bed of carefully placed white and black stones, surrounded by jars and bowls which had once held drink and food for the dead. Across the spinal column of the skeleton lay a beautifully preserved bronze dagger, which had once been attached to the belt which the man had worn.

From the first glance at the pottery in the tomb it was apparent that the burials belonged to that heyday of material culture in ancient Palestine known as the Hyksos period, or in more technical terms as the Middle Bronze II Age. In the doorway were two large, four-handle storage jars of a type that was widely used in the period; behind them were several beautifully made vases, with carinated profiles, and covered with a cream-like slip—obviously in imitation of metallic prototypes, probably of silver. Scattered here and there among the bones were little perfume juglets with a button-like base and a handle of two strands. Each of these forms is distinctive of the pottery of the Middle Bronze II period, now so well-documented by a large number of shaft tombs that have been found at Jericho. Since Diana Kirkbride had worked at Jericho as a tomb supervisor in 1953-1954, she was called from another part of the mound and asked to give her opinion of the date of Tomb 15. She observed that it could well have been a twin to any number of Middle Bronze II tombs at Jericho.

When Tomb 15 had been completely cleaned, the inventory of its contents amounted to 129 objects, which had been placed in the tomb for the fourteen people buried there. In addition to numerous bowls, plates, dipper juglets, perfume juglets, storage jars, there were two lamps—a rather small proportion of the total number of pottery vessels, in contrast to the heavy predominance of lamps found in the Iron Age tomb by Dajani in 1950. Three bronze dagger or knife blades were found, with rivets attached where a wooden handle had once been held in place, and two stone pommels for the handles of daggers. Four toggle pins, a gold ring, and nine scarabs constituted the jewelry of the tomb. There were only three beads and no earrings. It is not clear whether this conspicuous absence of rather common objects of personal adornment is evidence that only men were buried here or that the burials were of the poorer or more puritanical members of the community. A background of luxury, however, was suggested by the finding of twenty-four pieces of bone inlay from wooden boxes for toilet articles. These were decorated in a pleasing manner with incised circles and dots (Fig. 69).

Little could be learned about the offerings of food that had been placed within the tomb, except that there were four skulls of sheep or goats. Presumably, in addition to meat, provisions for the dead consisted of oil, wine, bread, and perhaps fruits and vegetables.

The picture of life at Gibeon in the Hyksos period provided by Tomb 15 was filled in with greater detail by material from twelve other tombs used during this period within the eighteenth-seventeenth centuries B.C. This seems to have been not only a time of general prosperity but one in which the arts and crafts flourished with a freshness and originality that had been introduced into Palestine by the arrival of a singularly creative group.

In contrast to the richness of the burials of the Middle Bronze II period was the comparative poverty evidenced by the tombs of the Middle Bronze I period. Burials of this period were accompanied by a few plain jars, and sometimes by a four-spouted lamp and a javelin point or a dagger. In each of the five tombs that contained some unmistakable tokens of the Middle Bronze I period there was evidence of reuse in the subsequent period. In one instance material from a burial made in the Late Bronze Age demonstrates the very long use of the tomb.

During the first three seasons of excavation at el-Jib the profile of occupation of the site had tallied nicely with the references to the city's history in the Bible, except for one puzzling, if not alarming discrepancy. According to the famous biblical account of the Gibeonites' covenant with Joshua and of the subsequent battle, in which Joshua defeated the Amorite coalition that laid siege to Gibeon, it is implied that at the time of the beginning of the conquest of Canaan by Israel the city was large and powerful enough to be at the head of a four-city league. Furthermore, it is explicitly stated in Joshua 10:2 that, "Gibeon was a great city, like one of the royal cities . . . and all its men were mighty." If the biblical account is historically reliable, and if the conquest of Canaan by a group of Israelites under Joshua took place in the thirteenth century—it is generally so dated—then there should be some evidence for the occupation of Gibeon in the Late Bronze period, which immediately preceded the Iron Age. It is not at all likely that "a great city" could have risen up suddenly just before Joshua's advance.

Yet in the first three seasons of work at el-Jib there had

not appeared any trace of occupation in the Late Bronze Age, a period of Palestine's history which is now known from an easily recognizable type of pottery. In this period pottery was elaborately decorated with paint in distinctive designs on forms that were at home in Greece and in Cyprus. Imported ware appears in the Late Bronze period along with local imitations of it. In our first three seasons this well-known type of ware had been conspicuously absent among the several hundred-thousands of sherds that had been retrieved and examined. Consequently, at the end of the 1959 campaign we had been forced to report that as yet not a trace of evidence had been found for any occupation at Gibeon during the Late Bronze period. From a fairly representative sampling of the mound at el-Jib it looked as though no material basis existed for "a great city" having been there at the time of Joshua.

This seeming discrepancy between the biblical record and the actual remains at the site was suddenly resolved in 1960, when we opened two tombs to find in them a rich assortment of Late Bronze Age pottery. That they were no isolated burials of the nomads of the period seems certain from the fact that one of them, Tomb 10B, had the largest number of objects (147 catalogued objects and 73 beads) that we have as yet found in a tomb at el-Jib. These richly furnished tombs of the Late Bronze period indicate that Gibeon was in existence in the period immediately before the time of Joshua, although we have thus far failed to find the particular area of the mound which the city of that period occupied.

The importance of this belated discovery of evidence for the Late Bronze occupation at Gibeon is heightened by the archaeological situation at the sites of two other cities mentioned in the biblical narratives dealing with the conquest of Joshua. At Jericho, which was the first objective of the conqueror, according to the account in the Book of Joshua, the archaeological evidence for occupation during the latter part of the Late Bronze Age is limited to a floor on which was found a small mud oven and a single dipper juglet, which can be dated to the fourteenth century B.C.[3] There were no houses and no city walls of this period; all the city, if it ever existed at all, has long since been washed down the slope of the hill.

At Ai the evidence for the period immediately before the conquest of the Israelites is lacking. The excavations of Mme. Judith Marquet-Krause at et-Tell, the most probable site for Ai, from 1933 to 1935, have demonstrated that there was a complete break in the occupation of the city from about 2000 to 1200 B.C. With such negative results from the excavation of two of the three cities mentioned prominently in the accounts of Joshua's conquest, the appearance at Gibeon of remains from this crucial period of Israel's history is of considerable significance for a reappraisal of the historical value of the narratives preserved in the first part of the Book of Joshua.

The contents of the Late Bronze Age tombs are of interest in themselves. In the pottery forms of this period there is material evidence for the contacts the Gibeonites of the day had with such a distant place as Cyprus. Ware imported from that island appears first in the Late Bronze period. The delicate skeuomorphic juglets of "base-ring" ware appear in some fine examples from the tombs (Fig. 65). The ware is unbelievably thin and painted with delicate lines of diagonal bands. The local imitations of this type of juglet are generally of heavier ware and the painting is not so delicately done. Lentoid flasks, or canteens, painted with concentric circles also appear in this period (Fig. 68). Paint is used effectively to decorate mugs with

[3] K. Kenyon, *Digging Up Jericho*, p. 261.

panels of complicated design (Figs. 66, 67) as well as for decorating the pyxis, a common type of small vessel with two lug handles. A rare example of a partly decomposed copper bowl appeared in the goods of Tomb 10A. The Late Bronze Age tombs also contained earrings, bracelets, scarabs, and other jewelry.

The decision of the Bronze Age peoples to locate their necropolis on the west side of the hill may have been dictated partly by the presence of a soft layer of limestone which could be hewn without too much effort. Another factor, however, may have been a less practical reason. Not only does the west side of the tell enjoy by far the most imposing view of the countryside surrounding el-Jib, but it is favored by a regular breeze from the Mediterranean which makes even the hottest summer day bearable. Although there is no material evidence for the conjecture, it is not impossible that the peoples of the Middle and Late Bronze periods, who took such pains to provide the dead with the necessities of food and drink, may also have sought to provide them with a permanent resting place that enjoyed a good view and a gentle, refreshing breeze during the hot summer months.

The most elaborately built tombs we have as yet found at Gibeon have been those associated with the Roman period of the city's history. We have already mentioned the thirty-four Roman tombs which had been robbed and which stood open around the sides of the hill when the Survey of Western Palestine was made.

Toward the end of the 1959 season we made an interesting rediscovery. While excavating in the second Industrial Area, where there had been a winery in the Iron II Age, we came upon what seemed at first to be a canal or water channel. It was a structure of two parallel walls of good masonry, plastered with lime plaster; and the width between them was about 4 feet. When we had traced the course of these two walls for a distance of 36 feet we came to a well-plastered cross wall. Obviously our first guess had been wrong: the structure could not be a canal.

Further excavation between the two parallel walls of this construction disclosed that it was a stairway, leading to the door of a large underground tomb. The entranceway is quite impressive (Fig. 105). After descending nine steps, one comes to a generous landing almost 10 feet in length; three more steps bring one to the entrance to the tomb, which lies 10 feet below the ground level.

The occasion of the opening of the doorway to the tomb was complicated by some delicate considerations of protocol. Who should be the first to enter? Since it was Hassan Abdullah's story about a cave and a sealed door which had brought us to this area only a few weeks before, he and his octogenarian friend el-Abushi were picked for the honor. All work stopped as these two bent figures, armed with flashlights, stooped to enter the door of the tomb and the entire labor force watched from the edge of the entranceway above. Then, after what seemed like an interminable period, the two old men emerged from the tomb with the reports of what they had seen. Protocol was strictly adhered to as Hasan Mamluk, the representative of the Jordanian Government, and then members of the staff, according to their seniority of experience in excavations, were allowed to enter. Finally at the lunch hour workmen were permitted to satisfy their curiosity as to the contents of this impressive burial chamber.

Alas, we had not been the first to discover this ancient mausoleum. As best we could judge from a tin gasoline can and a soup ladle of enameled ware, it was just about sixty years earlier—this had been the figure given by Hassan before we began to dig in his field—that someone had entered the tomb through an opening in the roof. Apparently the owner of the field had seen how his archaeological discovery could yield some practical benefit: this very large underground chamber was a convenient place in which to dispose of the stones that he wished to clear from his land. He had almost completely filled the tomb with several tons of field stones, closed the hole which he had made in the top, and then proceeded to cultivate a greatly improved plot of land.

At first we were staggered by the prospect of clearing away the stone pile. But by employing two shifts of men so that stones moved from 5:00 A.M. until 6:30 P.M. in two steady streams, one from the door of the tomb and the other from the hole in the roof, we managed to make the tomb once again habitable within a very few days. The results of the undertaking were well worth the effort. A large underground room, 26 by 13 feet, roughly rectangular in plan had been hewn from the rock. In the ceiling, about 7 feet 6 inches above the floor, four round openings in the rock can be seen, each capped over with stones and cemented with hard plaster on the outside (Fig. 52). These are the necks to four ancient wine cellars which had been enlarged to form the tomb chamber itself. In the floor of the tomb there are eleven loculi for individual burials. These vary slightly in size, but most are approximately 6 feet long, 2 feet wide, and from 3 to 4 feet deep. These burial vaults in the floor were originally covered with well-cut slabs of stone, approximately 3 feet by 1 foot 6 inches by 10 inches. These covers had been coated with thick plaster to provide a smooth floor for the tomb chamber. Within the loculi were pieces of the lead coffins, which had once contained the bodies, and lamps of the late Roman period.

Arcosolia, or burial niches, had been cut into the walls

of the tomb to provide for four more burials. The total number of graves in this mausoleum was fifteen. At other places in the walls of the tomb additional arcosolia had been marked out and the cutting begun (Fig. 107). But when the stone cutters had broken through into wine cellars which lay adjacent to the tomb they had ceased work. Obviously the tomb owners did not know of these cuttings in the rock which had fallen into disuse five or six centuries earlier.

When we had cleared the stairway leading down into the tomb we found that within the well-faced door jambs of the entrance there had been placed a crude, hastily built wall. The original door, a rectangular slab of limestone, 3 feet 5 inches by 2 feet 9 inches, was discovered lying on the floor of the tomb. The stone door had two projecting knobs to fit into the upper and the lower sockets to form the hinges upon which the door swung.

The unique feature of this tomb is the mural of paint and applied stucco which had once extended in a band around the upper part of the walls of the chamber (Fig. 106). The entire surface of the walls of the tomb had been first coated with a layer of off-white cement. On top of this, a second coat of cement, finer in texture and gray in color, had been applied. The ceiling had also once been plastered, but with the exception of one very small fragment all the plaster had fallen away.

The area of the walls which had been covered by the mural consists of a band 2 feet wide which extends from a point at about eye-level to the ceiling. This portion of the wall had first been coated with a beige wash and then painted dark blue. To this surface there were affixed the element of the design, which consisted of bas-relief stucco, or plaster, probably cast in a mold. The larger and heavier pieces of stucco were attached by means of iron nails driven into the wall, many of which still adhere (Fig. 107, upper right); the lighter elements were cemented to the surface of the wall by blobs of plaster or cement. An egg-and-dart mold, also cast, served as a lower border for the mural. None of the plaster work that was applied to the mural seems to have been painted. The design provided by the bas-relief stucco was supplemented by other elements painted upon the mural. Long, curling ribands of white paint served to decorate the stucco garlands. Other details were provided by yellow paint, an obvious imitation of gold.

Although we can be relatively certain of the technique that was employed in making the mural by a careful examination of the traces on the east wall of the tomb, we found it difficult to reconstruct the pattern of the design. According to village gossip many of the stucco reliefs had been stripped from the walls by those who had entered the tomb two generations earlier and had been reused to decorate the homes of the vandals. The reconstruction shown in Fig. 108 was made by Robert H. Smith, who placed a celluloid sheet over a series of enlarged photographs of the wall and traced upon it the preserved lines of the scene. From an intensive study of the details of plaster, the paint, and the nails driven into the wall, he observed that the mural consisted of repetitions of a basic pattern. Since some details of the repeated motif were found in one area and others in another, he was able, by shifting the celluloid overlay from one pattern to another, to reconstruct the entire scene with a convincing degree of accuracy.

The basic design consists of three elements: a garland of molded stucco, to which painted ribands appear to be tied; winged genii or cupids, which support the ends of the garlands; and a plaster head of Gorgon or Medusa, which appears in the hemispherical space within the garland. This motif of garland, winged genii, and head appears three times on the east wall of the tomb and in all probability was repeated along the walls to the south, west, and north. It is also probable that the egg-and-dart mold served as a border for this frieze around the walls of the tomb. The surface of the wall below the mural had been left free of decoration to allow for the cutting of arcosolia as they were needed for additional burials.

This type of tomb decoration is without parallel in Palestine, but the individual elements of the stucco and painted design appear in the funerary art of other parts of the Roman world, especially in the tradition of sarcophagus art that is known from the coastal region of Syria and Lebanon. A third-century painted tomb at Marwa[4] has the combination of garlands bedecked with ribands and gorgonea between them, but the genii are missing.

The lack of close parallels to this tomb and its decoration makes it difficult to fix its date. If the lamps found within the tomb are contemporaneous with the latter use of the tomb, then a date around A.D. 300 would be a reasonable guess for the decoration. The absence of any Christian or Jewish motifs, either upon the lamps or upon the tomb decoration, indicates that the tomb belonged to pagans, who are known to have used the garland-genius-gorgoneum motif in funerary art. Who the pagan Gibeonites were, who went to such pains to decorate this elaborate tomb, must remain for the present unanswered.

The tomb just described had been sealed off from an earlier tomb of an entirely different type. A portion of the west wall of the later tomb consists of a masonry wall behind which lies an oval chamber that had been made by the enlargement of two other wine cellars. In the walls of this oval-shaped room there are approximately two hundred neatly carved niches (Fig. 109), each of which measures approximately 8 inches high, 12 inches wide, and 8 inches deep. Similar funerary chambers, called columbaria, have

[4] *Quarterly of the Department of Antiquities in Palestine*, vol. 9, 1939, pp. 1-30.

been found in a number of places in Palestine. This burial arrangement served to accommodate the essential remains —probably ashes—of far more people than could possibly be interred in a tomb of the more traditional type. The entrance to the columbarium was probably to the south, an area that could not be excavated because of large trees.

Customs in burial practices exhibit some important changes over the long period for which we have evidence at el-Jib. The practice of the Early Bronze Age people in burying their dead in rock-cut caves in the side of the hill was abandoned at the beginning of the Middle Bronze period, when shaft tombs were first constructed. This distinctive type of tomb architecture continued through the Middle Bronze II period, when the endowment of the dead seems to have become the more elaborate, and throughout the Late Bronze Age. The Iron Age peoples again make use of caves in the scarp of the natural hill as places for burials and placed there the traditional funerary equipment. The one large tomb with such a high proportion of lamps belonging to the Iron Age is noteworthy. In the Roman period the monumental tomb becomes common. It is a large room, often with space for many burials and elaborate wall decoration. It would seem that the older practice of burying a full complement of articles of everyday life with the corpse was replaced by the use of coffins and by decoration upon the walls of the tomb.

Throughout this long period of changing burial customs the simple belief in the continued existence of life after death is constantly evidenced. Had not the Gibeonites believed so firmly in the continuance of life after death in the tomb we should know far less than we do today about the cultures of the major periods of the history of Gibeon and our museums would be without some of the best display pieces to illustrate what life was like in the important ages of the city's history.

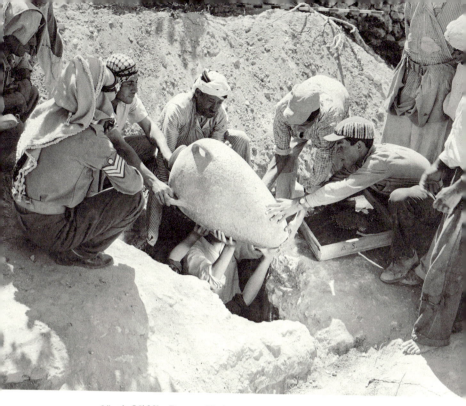

95. A Middle Bronze II Age storage jar is hoisted from Tomb 15 by workmen. At the left is the sergeant of the National Guard who checked on the guards of the tomb during the night. All dirt from the tomb was sifted through a fine screen in order to recover small objects. Contents of this tomb are diagramed in Fig. 99.

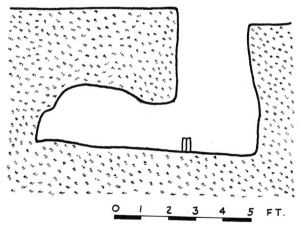

0 1 2 3 4 5 FT.

96. Section of a typical shaft tomb of the Bronze Age. A photograph of the shaft and door is shown in Fig. 104.

97. Draftsman Gustav Materna measures objects from a datum line stretched across Tomb 15.

98. In a tomb that had been completely silted up with soil washed in through crevices in the roof a boy removes the dirt from a burial with trowel and brush.

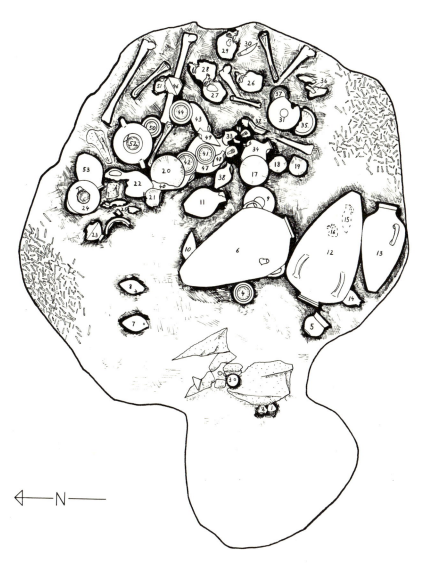

←—N—

99. Diagram of the upper layer of objects as they
were found in Tomb 15. The numbers are those by
which the objects were catalogued. In Fig. 95 storage jar 12 is shown being removed from the tomb.

100. A cylindrical shaft leading to Tomb 21. Quarry marks can be seen at the right of the opening.

101. A white steatite scarab with the cartouche of Amen-hotep II, from a tomb of the Late Bronze period.

102. A scarab bearing the name of Thut-mose III and a striding sphinx in the form of a lion with the head of the king wearing a false beard, wig, and uraeus.

103. The inside of a burial chamber after the contents had been removed. The doorway leads to a similar chamber, which is connected with yet another tomb chamber.

104. From the bottom of a circular shaft of a tomb of the Late Bronze Age a doorway leads into the burial chamber. Beside the trowel is a portion of the stone door which once sealed the tomb.

105. Entrance to the door of the Roman tomb.

107. A workman examines an unfinished b
niche in the wall of the tomb. The outline of a wi
genius of plaster which had once been attache
the wall by four nails can be seen at the upper ri

106. The doorway to the Roman tomb as seen from the inside. Remains of the mural can be seen at the upper right.

108. Reconstruction of a portion of the wall decoration within the tomb.

109. Niches for funerary remains cut into the wall of the columbarium.

110. A drawing of the Roman tomb and the columbarium.

CHAPTER VII

THREE THOUSAND YEARS
OF HISTORY

For many states that were once great have now become small;
and those that were great in my time were small formerly.
Knowing therefore that human prosperity never continues
in one stay, I will make mention alike of
both kinds.—HERODOTUS, Book I, 5

GIBEON is probably best known as the place where the sun stood still in obedience to Joshua's bold command. Besides this patently miraculous tale there are in the Bible accounts of dramatic events that have taken place at the city over a period of approximately six centuries. What historical data, if any, can be obtained from this collection of miraculous tales, heroic stories, and other biblical references to Gibeon?

If the Gibeonites ever wrote annals or a history of their city, they have long since been lost. All that remains of anything like a contemporary account of what happened there lies embedded in the heroic and religious history of Israel and in a few other ancient sources. The biblical stories are primarily concerned with the deeds of national heroes, such as Joshua, Saul, David, Joab, Abner, and Solomon, each of whom had a particular appeal to the folk memory and imagination of succeeding generations. Obviously beyond the range of historical confirmation are the hailstones that were said to have decimated Israel's foes at the battle of Gibeon, the staying of the sun for a whole day, and the pool of blood from the slain Amasa in the highway near Gibeon. These and other incidents of popular tradition serve to embroider the history of Gibeon and to suggest the city's prominence in the life of ancient Israel; but they cannot be used in the writing an account of how men lived in the city.

Although many of the stories themselves are entirely beyond the range of confirmation they have preserved bits of information which, when sifted out, can be utilized by the historian in the construction of a framework for a history. Surely Gibeon was a considerable city at the time of the writing—or the period of the formation of the oral tradition later committed to writing—of the stories of Joshua's conquests. In David's day there must have existed at Gibeon a great pool that was such a widely recognized landmark that it could be cited as the locale of the decisive contest between the men of Joab and the men of Abner. Incidental allusions to Gibeon such as these are not without their historical value.

The discovery of four Hebrew letters scratched on the handle of a wine jar gave a unique dimension to the excavations at el-Jib. The appearance of the name Gibeon at the site under circumstances that made it possible to identify el-Jib with the ancient biblical city affords an opportunity both to test by archaeology the outline of Gibeon's history, as it can be reconstructed from the scattered references in the Bible, and to supplement it with a wealth of significant detail that biblical writers took for granted.

In contrast to the colorful and dramatic character of the biblical narratives about heroes and villains, the archaeological results are less specific and relatively unexciting. Excavation has yielded information principally about successive layers of occupation, which can be dated fairly accurately—city walls, houses, artifacts, tombs, and a great variety of evidence as to how the average man lived in each of the periods of the city's history. Occasionally, however, the anonymity of the archaeological evidence is broken by the appearance of writing. More than 150 individual pieces of writing on stone, clay, or bronze have been found in four seasons of excavations. From the fifteenth century B.C. through the seventh century A.D., no less than six different scripts were employed in writing: Egyptian hieroglyphs, archaic Hebrew, Aramaic, Greek, Latin, and Arabic. We have found writings in each of these characters.

This valuable information about the history of the city and its people consists almost exclusively of names. In addition to the thirty occurrences of the name of the city itself, there appear the names of neighboring cities: Hebron, Socoh, Ziph, Mozah, and Memshath, all of which, with the exception of the last, are known from the Bible. On scarabs or on coins are the names of such well-known historical figures as Thut-mose III, Amen-hotep II, John Hyrcanus I, Alexander Jannaeus, Herod the Great, Nero, Herod Agrippa, and the seventh century Byzantine Emperor Heraclius. Other coins have been found from the mints of Ptolemy II Philadelphus, Antiochus III, Pontius Pilate, Domitian, Gallienus, Constantine I, and Constans II.

The actual names of some of the citizens of Gibeon in the seventh and sixth centuries B.C. are known to us either from impressions on clay or from graffiti on jar handles. For the most part they bear names that are known from the Bible, such as Hananiah, Azariah, Amariah, and Meshullam. In these discoveries we have another sure tie between the biblical record and the results of archaeology.

In the present chapter we will seek to present a synthesis of the biblical and archaeological evidence and to sketch the history of the six cities and the two periods of settlement at Gibeon. The actual remains found at el-Jib carry us far back beyond the earliest biblical reference; for Gibeon was a city for almost 2,000 years before the first mention of it in the Bible. Admittedly there are gaps in the long record, which extends from the first urban settlement at about 3000 B.C. down through Roman times, yet we have been able to fill in some of them by drawing upon results of other excavations at neighboring sites in Palestine to which our findings at el-Jib are connected by unmistakable clues.

Gibeon first became a city at the beginning of the Early Bronze Age, about 5,000 years ago. Long before the beginning of this period of extensive urban settlement in Palestine when the land was well populated with fortified city-states, scattered groups of people probably settled in the region of the spring of Gibeon to take advantage of the water and the fertility of the surrounding fields. But evidence for settlements in the Neolithic and Chalcolithic periods is as yet completely lacking. The earliest remains that we have found anywhere on the hill are those of a city of well-built houses which extended over a considerable part of the mound.

Our discovery of the Early Bronze Age city was quite unexpected; in fact it was made long before we had found the foundations for some of the buildings of later periods of occupation. When we had come upon the city wall of the Iron Age in 1956, we began to dig a trench into the debris that had accumulated against its outside face for the purpose of determining, if possible, the time of its construction and the history of its use. Layers of debris made up of refuse thrown over the wall, we assumed, should reveal some clues about the length of time it had served as a fortified boundary for the city. It was here, while looking for what information we could gather about the history of the city wall, that we encountered the floor of a storeroom below the level of the foundations of the fortification. On the hard, beaten earth were fourteen storage jars; each had been crushed into a neat pile of sherds by the collapse of the roof of the house when the wooden beams which had spanned the stone walls had burned. This evidence bore mute testimony of a catastrophe which had come suddenly upon the owner of the house.

By piecing together these broken jars we were able to identify them as being similar in type to jars which were in common use in the Early Bronze Age. The jars had flat bases, from which the walls of the vessel rose almost perpendicularly. The potter had used a wheel, but it was a slow wheel which merely enabled him to smooth the sides and the rim of the vessel as it was turned; the fast wheel, which made it possible for the potter to throw a mass of clay into a symmetrical vessel, had obviously not yet been devised.

The most distinctive feature of the vessels remains even yet a puzzle. On the shoulder there is a pillar-like handle with a concave impression in the top of it. This rounded impression is much too large to have been intended as a support for the thumb of the hand as it grasped the handle, and it is too small to have supported a juglet which was used to dip out the contents of the jar. It may be that this impractical handle is the vestige of some functional feature of the jars of an earlier age from which we have no surviving examples. The finding of this peculiar handle makes it possible to connect this earliest settlement at el-Jib with those of the Early Bronze Age at such neighboring places as Ai, seven miles to the northeast, Tell en-Nasbeh, just three miles to the north, and Jericho, in the Jordan Valley some sixteen miles to the east.

Pottery and house walls of the Early Bronze period have

been found at the highest point on the mound, where the stratification had been destroyed by British gunfire in the campaign of General Allenby in 1917. A tomb on the east side of the hill has supplied further evidence for life at Gibeon in the period by producing considerable unbroken pottery and some personal effects. Sun-baked bricks of mud, made in a mold which was 3½ inches deep and 16 inches wide, have been found associated with the pottery of the period. The walls from which the bricks came were standing for only a course or two and there was every indication that they had been destroyed by fire.

It is highly probable that Gibeon, like its neighbors in this period, was surrounded by a strong city wall, although no trace of it has yet been uncovered. The finding of a room full of storage jars makes it certain that Gibeon was something more than a camping place in this period when Palestine was a land of well-fortified city-states.

The Palestine of the Early Bronze period, when Gibeon was an important city, is now fairly well known from remains of about a dozen cities which flourished at various times within the thousand years of this prosperous era. At strategic points throughout the land farmers lived in rectangular houses built up solidly within massive city walls, which sometimes reached a thickness of 28 feet, as they did at Tell el-Farah. Although the designation of Early Bronze has been given to this cultural period by archaeologists, bronze or copper was actually relatively scarce; tools and weapons were fashioned chiefly of flint. There is not the slightest evidence to show that bows and arrows were used for the defense of the city; stones hurled from the walls were probably the only means for driving away attackers from the outside. To judge from the charred wood found in excavations and from the post holes found in rooms, it is likely that wood was widely used in buildings. One competent archaeologist has ventured the theory that this prosperous period in Palestine's history came to its end because of the deforestation which this generous use of wood in construction occasioned.

The best-preserved evidence of the Early Bronze period is an abundance of pottery. The forms are graceful and well made, thanks to the development in this period of an adequate means for firing the clay vessels. At Tell el-Farah a pottery kiln of the Early Bronze period has been unearthed. It has two chambers, one for the fire and another for the oven; flues served to conduct the heat from the chamber where the wood burned to the oven filled with vessels. Decoration in the form of hand burnishing and of delicate patterns in paint was widely used on a rich variety of forms. The earliest potter's wheel yet to be discovered has come from a stratum of this period at Beth-yerah in the upper Jordan Valley.

On the whole the picture of life in this phase of Palestine's history is one of prosperity and relative simplicity. There seems to have been no strong central power in the land; each city-state was an independent unit, well-fortified to keep out the nomadic invaders who continually pressed in from the desert and to maintain its own independence. Gibeon participated in this highly satisfactory way of life which flourished in Palestine during the third millennium B.C.

Five of the shaft tombs cut in the rock at el-Jib have provided some conclusive evidence for the history of Gibeon following the end of the Early Bronze period. The amount of material from this relatively obscure period is admittedly small: four small, but very distinctive jars, four examples of a lamp with four nozzles, and a beautifully preserved javelin point of bronze with a curled tang by which it was once attached to a wooden shaft. The pottery jars are of a type that has thus far been found only in tombs, and it seems likely that the vessel was one intended for the dead rather than for the living. It is a tall, barrel-like jar with a slightly flaring rim. The body was made by hand, but the rim was fashioned on a slow wheel. Bands of delicate combing appear on the shoulder; the ware is buff in color and extremely brittle. It seems unfitted for any use other than decoration.

Although the burials were disturbed by those who reused the tombs in subsequent periods, the later users left in each of them some tokens of the Middle Bronze I Age. The picture of the culture of these settlers at Gibeon at the very beginning of the Middle Bronze period, who left this scant but unmistakable evidence, can now be filled in with information that has come from the tombs of the same people found at Jericho between 1952 and 1954. No less than 65 tombs of this type were excavated there by Kathleen M. Kenyon.

The burial customs of the Middle Bronze I settlers differ from those of their urban predecessors of the Early Bronze Age. Each tomb contained only one burial in contrast to the multiple burials of the earlier period. The body was placed in the tomb after the flesh had decayed and the skeleton had become completely or largely disarticulated. At Jericho the excavators were able to detect clear evidence for this rare custom of bringing the bones of the skeleton into the tomb in a basket from termite tracks which could be seen on the floor of the tomb. Professor F. E. Zeuner's note on this important deduction about burial customs from termite tracks is of interest:

This container [a basket of woven reeds or other fiber] was almost certainly left behind with the bones. Some

time after the tomb had been closed, termites pene-
trated to the chamber, entering through a fissure at
330°, building a corridor straight down to the floor
and across to the skeleton. Since termites do not eat
animal matter, vegetable material must at one time
have been associated with the skeleton and been eaten
up by them. In the process some bones became covered
with crumbs of earth used by the termites in con-
structing their covering alleys. When no more edible
matter was left, the termites withdrew.[1]

The tombs generally had but a limited repertoire of
simple pots; a four-spouted lamp, which was placed in a
niche cut into the wall, bronze pins, beads, spindle-whorls,
and stone objects made up the collection of rather meager
tomb-goods.

These relics of the Middle Bronze I people seem to
indicate a fresh migration into the town of a nomadic people
who brought with them an entirely new tradition in pottery
forms and new customs in burial practices. They may have
come into Palestine from the desert at the crossing of the
Jordan near Jericho and may then have pushed on to settle
eventually at such places as Gibeon, Tell el-Ajjul, and
Lachish, where tombs of this distinctive type have been
found. Although no javelin points were found in the tombs
of this type at Jericho, both Tell el-Ajjul and Lachish have
yielded examples of the javelin point with curled tang
which are identical with the one found in the Middle Bronze
I tomb at Gibeon (Fig. 72).

Since these Middle Bronze I newcomers into Palestine
at Jericho camped at the site without the protection of a city
wall and only later built houses, it is quite probable that
they lived at Gibeon in similar temporary quarters. It is

[1] Kathleen M. Kenyon, *Excavations at Jericho*, vol. 1, 1960,
p. 219.

difficult to place the advent of these settlers precisely in time; perhaps they are best fitted into the twenty-first and twentieth centuries.

What may be labeled as the second city to have stood on the mound at el-Jib belongs to the Middle Bronze II or the Hyksos period. This urban occupation in the eighteenth and seventeenth centuries B.C. is documented by the remains of a house that lay beneath about 13 feet of accumulated debris at the northwest of the site. When Diana Kirkbride first encountered this room in 1960 she removed a foot of ashes, charcoal, and burnt bricks to discover 16 large storage jars crushed in the positions they had occupied on the day when the beams and supporting post of the roof had burned in what doubtlessly was a disastrous destruction. Fortunately the post that supported a long span of the roof had been set in a circular hole in the dirt floor. Although the upper part of the post had burned completely in the conflagration, the buried portion had smoldered and turned to charcoal. A careful examination of fragments of the charred post by the U.S. Forest Products Laboratory in Madison, Wisconsin, has made it certain that the support for this house was the trunk of an olive tree.

The pottery from this house is of a well-known type. Since sherds of it have been found at widely separated points over the mound, the area of occupation must have been extensive in this period. The best picture of life and culture at Gibeon in the Middle Bronze II period comes, however, not from the everyday remains of the living but from the generous gifts of grave-goods with which the dead were supplied. In 1960 we found tombs of the Hyksos period which revealed a cross section of the sophisticated arts and crafts of that day. So distinctive are the types of pottery, bronze objects, and scarabs that it is possible to

THREE THOUSAND YEARS OF HISTORY

match them up with a mass of evidence which has appeared elsewhere at such neighboring city-states as Jericho, Tell el-Ajjul, Lachish, and others.

The best pottery ever made at Gibeon throughout more than 3,000 years was produced by the potters of the Middle Bronze II city. Jars and bowls were thrown on a fast wheel in delicate and artistically pleasing shapes. The walls were thin and the ware was fired to a metallic hardness. A natural mistake made by a cataloguer in 1960 will illustrate how fine and delicate this ware is. A portion of an ostrich eggshell was found in one of the tombs. It was placed on the shelf with pieces of broken pottery where it remained for almost a year without being recognized for what it actually was. Never in succeeding periods did the Gibeonite potters exhibit this skill in producing such a wide repertoire of exquisite pottery.

Metal, which had been used in the Early Bronze period only sparingly, was widely used in the Hyksos period for daggers, rings, toggle pins, earrings, and other purposes. Cosmetic boxes of wood were inlaid with carved bone on which were representations of birds and geometric designs. Although all evidence for wooden objects had evidently decayed in the Gibeon tombs, the corresponding tombs at Jericho contained tables, stools, wooden bowls, and other furniture. The best evidences for dating the remains of this city are a number of Egyptian scarabs, some of them handsomely mounted in gold and bronze rings.

During the Middle Bronze II period at Gibeon the material culture reached a level of artistic sophistication which is unique in the long history of the city. The Gibeonite city of this period is contemporary with the great empire of Hammurabi in Babylon, but there is no evidence of either trade or military contact with this eastern power. Gibeon was evidently an independent city-state, free for a time from Egyptian domination during the period of the Hyksos rule in the Delta.

If the Gibeon of the Hyksos period may be termed sophisticated in its artistic attainments, particularly in ceramic forms, then it is appropriate to speak of its successor in the Late Bronze period as cosmopolitan. It is in this period, more than in any other of the city's history, that one encounters a wide variety of imported artifacts from such distant points as Egypt in the south and Cyprus in the west. A tomb in which seven citizens of the Late Bronze Age had been buried contained a beautifully cut steatite scarab bearing the name of Amen-hotep II in hieroglyphics (Fig. 101). This Egyptian monarch, who ruled from 1447 to 1421 B.C., made two campaigns into Palestine and carried away prisoners and booty. Although only a few of the towns that he took can be identified from the boastful accounts of his conquests, it is of interest that he records the taking of 36,300 Kharu, or Horites, the very term used in Joshua 9:7, according to the Greek version, for the Gibeonites. Another tomb had within it a scarab of Thut-mose III (about 1490-1436 B.C.), who for twenty years led campaigns almost every year into Asia (Fig. 102).

From Cyprus the Gibeonites of the Late Bronze period imported jugs, probably filled with perfumed oil. This distinctive jug, sometimes called a "bilbil," has a globular body surmounted by a long neck and a handle which springs gracefully from the shoulder to the mouth of the vessel. The ware is hard and thin and is usually decorated with lines of white, red, and black paint. A few broken examples of this "base-ring" ware, as it is called, make it clear that the handle was joined to the body of the jug by first punching a round hole in the body and then inserting the handle so that a portion of it projected through into the inside of the vessel. The Palestinians frequently imitated this type of jug but they never used the distinctive Cypriote technique in attaching the handle. The Cypriote jug never rises up straight from its base but always stand slightly askew with a kind of graceful lilt.

We are not dependent solely upon artifacts for the history of Palestine in the Late Bronze period. For almost the entire period of three centuries the city-states of Palestine were under the control of Egypt, whose kings made periodic expeditions to the region to the north to keep the rulers of the cities loyal. Although few texts in Canaanite have survived from this period, Egyptian royal annals in hieroglyphics carved ostentatiously on the walls of public buildings and a remarkable diplomatic correspondence in cuneiform found at Tell el-Amarna provide a rich embroidery of detail for the history of this period. Under Egyptian domination the cities of Palestine were participants in world trade as it passed along the roads that ran north and south through the land. At el-Jib we have found ample evidence of Gibeon's participation in the international trade of this period.

It is at the end of the Late Bronze period, late in the thirteenth century, that the earliest biblical reference to Gibeon must be placed. The Gibeonites emerge first on the biblical scene as the wily deceivers of Joshua, the leader of the conquest by which Israel came into control of certain principal cities of Palestine. Since Gibeon is described as "a great city" at this time, one would expect to find city walls and houses if the tradition preserved in the Book of Joshua is historically trustworthy. Yet traces of this city of the latter part of the Late Bronze period have not come to light in the four seasons of excavations. The two richly furnished tombs of the period discovered on the west side of the mound in 1960 would seem to indicate that somewhere on the mound itself there was a permanent settlement. Tombs filled with articles that had been imported from distant lands are not likely to have been those belonging to nomadic tribes which camped on the site. Perhaps in an area not yet excavated—to date we have dug into but a fraction of the total area—the remains of the "great city" of Joshua's day are to be found.

The biblical traditions that describe how the Israelites established themselves in the land of Canaan during the two centuries from the end of the conquest of Joshua to the time of David are completely silent about the great city and the mighty men who made a covenant of peace with the invaders. As far as we know the Gibeonites did not come to the aid of Israel's judges in the succession of crises for Israel which arose in their struggle for the control of the land. Nor were the Gibeonites ever mentioned in the Book of Judges as the allies of the foes of Israel. At the end of the period there is the single reference to an attack that Saul made upon the people of Gibeon but no details are given as to when or for what reason Israel's first king put the Gibeonites to death. It is clear, however, that in the days of David, Saul's successor, the Gibeonites had not been fully assimilated into the group of tribes that were finally absorbed into the kingdom. It was only during David's rule that they became a part of Israel and its cult; in the following generation Solomon could make use of the high place of Gibeon without the slightest impropriety.

The archaeological remains for the city during the days of Israel's judges are considerable, despite the leveling off of many buildings in the Iron II period, the heyday of Gibeon's prosperity and expansion. Pottery that is distinctive of the Iron I period has been found in areas both on the west and the east sides of the tell, and there is evidence that the earlier phase of the city wall immediately over the spring was in use during a good part of the two centuries before the time of David. The general impression of the culture of the period is one of artistic decadence and even poverty. In the tomb that Dajani excavated on the east side of the hill in 1950, pottery and artifacts of the Iron I period were found in abundance. The forms of the vessels that had been placed in the tomb were monotonous and even crude when compared to the ware of the two earlier periods in the city's history. The delicately wrought forms of bronze weapons are replaced by crude shapes in iron. Both the sophistication of the Middle Bronze II period and the urbanity of the Late Bronze period are replaced in the Iron I Age by a culture that is decidedly lacking in luster.

The Gibeonites of the first Iron Age did, however, distinguish themselves through a remarkable feat of engineering. For it was in this period that the great pool was planned as a measure of civil defense. Some strong ruler was able to impound enough laborers to bring to completion this project that entailed the quarrying and removal of approximately 3,000 tons of limestone.

Is this spectacular monument the famous "pool of Gibeon" mentioned in II Samuel 2:13 as the scene of the contest between the men of Joab and the men of Abner? Since this bout was between the forces of two contestants for the throne of Israel, it is likely that it took place on some neutral ground that was accessible to both forces. This proper assumption has led students of this ancient narrative to look for the pool of the contest in some area within the plain and not upon the mound, which was certainly fortified in this period. The large pool to the east of the spring of the village of el-Jib has often been cited as the scene of the battle in the days of David's struggle for the throne of a united Israel. The difficulty, however, with placing the site of the pool of Gibeon in this unprotected area is that a pool of water in the unfortified plain would have been of little use to the Gibeonites in an era when hostile armies and other enemies made high city walls necessary. A pool outside would have been an easy target for destruction or pollution by any enemy, and water carriers from the city would have been easy marks for the besiegers of the city. The site of the "pool of Gibeon," must, therefore, be sought within the fortified area of the city and not outside it.

We have found that in the Iron I period, to which the story of the contest must be assigned, the area around the great pool at el-Jib was completely free of buildings. There would have been sufficient room in the open square for the two dozen men who were involved in the contest as well as for a considerable number of spectators. They could well have sat down beside the pool, the "one on the one side of the pool, and the other on the other side of the pool."

The Hebrew word *berekhah*, used in the account for "pool," would not have been inappropriate as a designation for the cylindrical cutting in the shape of a pool, even though it merely served at the time to provide access to the spring of water lying 80 feet below the surface. Indeed, it is not unlikely that a landmark such as this remarkable construction should have remained firmly attached to the tradition of the gruesome contest between the men of Joab and the men of Abner, as firmly attached to the event as the place name Gibeon itself. Obviously, certainty of identification is impossible, but it is not improbable that we have in the pool at el-Jib an example of the unearthing of a monument which is specifically mentioned in the pages of the Old Testament.

A second engineering project that was probably completed within this period was the cutting of the stepped tunnel leading from the city to the spring at the base of the hill. It is evident from a study of the plans made of the two systems for supplying the city with water that the tunnel was devised after the cutting of the great pool and the building of the second phase of the city wall. Provisionally we suggest the tenth century as the most likely time for the construction of the stepped tunnel; it remained in use for many centuries as the principal access to the water of the spring.

A new epoch in the history of Gibeon may be said to have begun with the division of the empire of Solomon into the two kingdoms of Israel and Judah at the end of the tenth century. Gibeon lay at first in the contested territory of Benjamin but eventually it came under the control of the Judaean king in Jerusalem. Written records that mention the city are lacking from the latter part of the tenth century, when Gibeon is mentioned in the list of Sheshonk, until the end of the seventh century, when the name again appears as the home of the prophet Hananiah. For the period of these dark ages of the city's history some information can be had from the records of the kingdom of Judah, to which Gibeon belonged; but our principal source for this period is archaeology, which fortunately provides us with entirely new material about the economy and culture of the city and the names of some of its citizens.

If Sheshonk took Gibeon, as he claims to have done on his march northward in the fifth year of Rehoboam, he apparently did little damage to its city walls and buildings. No evidence has appeared thus far for a general destruction by fire within either the Iron I or the Iron II periods. Apparently the city continued to grow and develop throughout these two ages of its history without any marked disruption of its normal life.

The frequent invasions of Assyrian kings in the eighth

and seventh centuries apparently bypassed the city. In Isaiah 10:28-32 there appears the itinerary of a foreign invader as he made his way southward to attack Jerusalem. If this was the usual route of the Assyrian conquerors they would have passed several miles to the east of Gibeon on their march toward the capital of the Judaean kingdom.

Evidence for what was probably an unsuccessful attack upon Gibeon in the seventh century was discovered in 1960. It is a delicately fashioned bronze arrowhead with three sharp flanges or blades. At the base of this arrowhead, slightly more than an inch and a half long, there is a socket for the shaft of the arrow and a hole for the pin which held it securely. Since this rare type of arrowhead has been found in the graves of South Russia of the seventh century B.C. it is generally believed that the few examples found in Palestine are to be associated with the invasions of the Scythians who are described by Herodotus or with the "evil from the north," whose "quiver is like an open tomb," as described by Jeremiah. The sharpness of the blades of this unique type of bronze arrowhead might well have served to terrify the inhabitants of Judah at the end of the seventh century.

The period of three centuries for which we have no ancient historical records—or even allusions to the city— was a time of unrivaled prosperity and general expansion for the city. The defensive wall, which completely encircled the tell, was maintained and houses with foundations frequently placed on the bedrock were constructed over most of the area. A thriving industry in the making and distribution of wine, which was exported under the "Gibeon" label, undoubtedly contributed to the general prosperity. Evidence for contacts with neighboring towns—such as royal jar stamps and impressions of private seals—seems to suggest a picture of lively commercial activity which reached a peak in the seventh century.

Throughout the period of the divided monarchy in Israel Gibeon continued to prosper as a city of commerce. Only one prophet is mentioned as having come from Gibeon—and he was a false prophet. Perhaps such prosperity as the city enjoyed was not the catalyst to produce an Amos, or an Isaiah, or a Jeremiah.

There is every indication that the prosperous era for Gibeon came to a sudden end at the beginning of the Babylonian exile. Huge stones from the city wall had been hurled down into the pool to clog the water supply at the beginning of the sixth century; after this impairment of the city's defenses Gibeon ceased to be a city. Certainly the city wall was never again rebuilt. So slightly did the debris of later occupants of the site cover the mound that even today one can pick up sherds of the Iron II period which are constantly plowed out by the Arab farmers who work the land.

During the Persian and the Hellenistic periods Gibeon was not completely deserted. Jar handles stamped with the name Mozah, written in the Aramean script of the Persian period, evidence some settlement here during the fifth century. A few coins bearing the impressions of Ptolemy II Philadelphus, Antiochus III, and John Hyrcanus I have been found, but the remains of the Hellenistic period are scant indeed. These and other relics of broken pottery suggest only scattered and sporadic settlements on the mound during the Persian and Hellenistic periods.

Early in the first century B.C. Gibeon was again inhabited extensively, but this time it was an open city without an encircling wall. The settlement was over an extended area. Well-plastered baths with steps leading down to the pool were constructed in several places. Some of the ancient wine cellars of the Iron II period were cleaned, plastered, equipped with curb stones, and reused as cisterns for water. The ancient landmark of the city, the pool of Gibeon, which had long since been filled with debris, was forgotten, although the tunnel leading from the summit of the hill to the spring was probably used as a convenient access to the principal water supply. A large reservoir was built in the plain to the east of the spring to catch and to contain the overflow from the spring in the rainy season. The prosperity of the city in this last phase of its life is best evidenced by the elaborate tomb which was carved out of six ancient wine cellars and decorated with a sophisticated design of molded plaster and paint.

Gibeon had a long and relatively peaceful history. Only occasionally did sudden destruction come upon its inhabitants throughout the period of more than 3,000 years during which men drew water from the constantly flowing spring, tilled the rich fields which surround the hill, enjoyed the cool, refreshing breezes which blow regularly from the Mediterranean, and buried their dead along the terraces of the rock on the side of the tell. When one considers the warfare and destruction which are known to have taken place elsewhere in Palestine over these three millennia—the conquests of the Egyptian kings of the New Kingdom, the invasions of Hebrews and Philistines, the destructions by the Assyrians, the conquests of the Babylonians, and the civil wars in Israel—it is surprising that Gibeon bears so few scars. Possibly one explanation is its geographical position: the city was not on the main route of the principal invasions of the land. Another explanation may be that found in the tradition which has been preserved in the Book of Joshua. Once when Gibeon was threatened, its elders made peace with the invader and thus saved their city from destruction. Is it not possible that the people of Gibeon, so clever and adept at compromise on this one remembered occasion, may have used similar tactics to meet other threats to their security? Whether they were fortunate in their geographical location or whether they were particularly gifted at diplomacy—and perhaps even compromise and deception—the fact remains that the Gibeonites managed to live at peace for a good portion of their long history.

APPENDIX

THE STAFF AT EL-JIB

Gerald Cooke, cataloguer, 1960
Robert C. Dentan, supervisor, 1956
Asia G. Halaby, cataloguer, 1957, 1959; supervisor, 1960
T. Hartley Hall, IV, photographer and supervisor, 1956
Mohammed Hasan, supervisor, 1960
John Huesman, S.J., supervisor, 1959
Claus-Hunno Hunzinger, epigrapher, 1957
Jean H. Johnson, cataloguer, 1956
Sherman E. Johnson, administrative director, 1956
Diana Kirkbride, supervisor, 1960
Arnulf Kuschke, supervisor, 1960
Gustav Materna, draftsman, 1959, 1960
Hasan Mamluk, supervisor, 1959
Robert J. Marshall, supervisor, 1959
John L. McKenzie, S.J., supervisor, 1960
Subhi Muhtadi, surveyor, 1956, 1957, 1959, 1960
Willard Oxtoby, supervisor, 1959
Marvin Pope, supervisor, 1959
James B. Pritchard, director, 1956, 1957, 1959, 1960
Sally Pritchard, supervisor, 1960
William L. Reed, supervisor, 1959
H. Neil Richardson, supervisor, 1956, 1959
Marcia Rogers, architect, 1956
R. B. Y. Scott, cataloguer, 1959
Mohammed Shehadeh, draftsman, 1959
Kenneth Short, supervisor, 1960
Robert H. Smith, supervisor, 1959

Choan-seng Song, supervisor, 1959
Douglas M. Spence, supervisor, 1959
Thorir Thordarson, supervisor, 1956
Fred V. Winnett, supervisor, 1957, 1959
Linda A. Witherill, draftsman, 1957.

CHRONOLOGY

OF PRELIMINARY REPORTS

T H E following preliminary reports and news accounts of the excavations have appeared:

1956: *New York Times*, Sept. 9, 1956; *Illustrated London News*, Oct. 27, 1956, pp. 695-697; *Biblical Archaeologist*, vol. 19, no. 4, Dec. 1956, pp. 66-75; *University Museum Bulletin*, vol. 21, no. 1, March 1957, pp. 3-26.

1957: *New York Times*, Sept. 21, 1957; *Time*, Oct. 7, 1957, p. 74; *Saturday Evening Post*, Feb. 8, 1958, pp. 40-41, 87-90; *Illustrated London News*, Mar. 29, 1958, pp. 505-507; *University Museum Bulletin*, vol. 22, no. 2, June 1958, pp. 13-24; *Christianity Today*, June 9, 1958, pp. 3-4.

1959: *New York Times*, Sept. 27, 1959; *Expedition*, vol. 2, no. 1, Fall, 1959, pp. 17-25; *Supplement to Vetus Testamentum*, vol. 7, Leiden, 1960, pp. 1-12; *Biblical Archaeologist*, vol. 23, no. 1, Feb. 1960, pp. 23-29; *Illustrated London News*, Sept. 10, 1960, pp. 433-435.

1960: *The Times*, London, July 23, 1960; *Time*, Aug. 8, 1960, p. 69; *Illustrated London News*, Sept. 24, 1960, pp. 518-519; *Bulletin of the American Schools of Oriental Research*, no. 160, Dec. 1960, pp. 2-6; *Biblical Archaeologist*, vol. 24, no. 1, Feb. 1961, pp. 19-24; *Expedition*, vol. 3, no. 4, Summer, 1961, pp. 2-9.

INDEX

━━━━━━━━━ ☆ ━━━━━━━━━

lion's head, 122
loom weight, 106, 114

mace head, 113
McKenzie, John L., 10, 169
Mahanaim, 35
Mahmud Ahmed Hussein, 128
Makkedah, 33
Marquet-Krause, Judith, 4, 137
Marshall, Robert J., 169
Marwa, 143
Materna, Gustav, 10, 132, 169
Mazar, B., 42n
Medusa, 142
Megiddo, 64, 122
Memshath, 117, 147
Mephi-bosheth, 38
Mereru-ka, 97
Merob, 38
Meshullam, 120, 147
metal, 112-17
mills, 106
Mizpah, 41
Mohammed Hasan, 10, 169
Mohammed Shehadeh, 169
mortars, 85-86
Mozah, 147, 163
Muhtadi, Subhi, 10-11, 169
Mycenae, 64

Nahum, 120
Nakht, 97
Nebi Samwil, 39, 88
Nebuchadnezzar, 40, 53, 71
necropolis, see tombs
needles, 114
Nero, 147
Nicropolis, 44

Og, 31
olive press, 84
olive tree, 154
Onomasticon, 28-29, 43-44
Osiris, 122
ostrich eggshell, 155
ovens, 107
Oxtoby, Willard, 169

Palestine Archaeological Museum, 127-28
palette, 116
Paula, 28
pay day, 20
Petrie, Sir Flinders, 21
place names, 26-27, 120

plow, 113-14
Pococke, Richard, 29
Pontius Pilate, 147
pool-and-stairway, 64-70, 73, 159, 163, 164; plan and section, 69; date of cutting, 71-72; date of filling, 70
"pool of Gibeon," 35-36, 53, 74, 76, 159-60
Pope, Marvin, 169
potter's wheel, 109, 151
pottery, 108-12, 155; recording of, 10; kiln, 151
Pritchard, James B., 169
Pritchard, Sally, 169
Ptolemy II Philadelphus, 147, 163

quarry, 102-3
Qumran, 77

Rainey, Froelich, 14
Ramses III, 102
recording, 10, 132-33
Reed, William L., 10, 169
Rehoboam, 42, 161
religion, 120-22
rental of land, 16-18
reservoirs, 74-78, 164
Richardson, H. Neil, 10, 87, 169
rings, 116
ring-stands, 112
Rizpah, 29, 37-38
Robinson, Edward, 24-29, 43, 52, 54, 74
Rogers, Marcia, 169
roof, 107, 154
royal stamps, 87, 106, 117-18

Said Durra, 16
Sakkarah, 97
Samuel, 107
Saul, 29-30, 35, 37-39, 41, 53, 100, 107, 145, 158
scarabs, 155-56
Schick, Baurath C., 54
Scott, R. B. Y., 83-84, 88, 169
Scythians, 162
seals, 119-20
Sennacherib, 71
Seti I, 46, 102
settling basin, 98
shafts for light, 70
Shakr Abd el-Hamid, 128
Sheba, 36-37
Shebuel, 48, 51